HOLD FAST
YOUR DREAMS

HOLD FAST YOUR DREAMS

Twenty Commencement Speeches

CARRIE BOYKO AND KIMBERLY COLEN

SCHOLASTIC INC.
New York Toronto London Auckland Sydney
Mexico City New Delhi Hong Kong

To my husband,
Alan, and my kids:
Marc — Class of 2005
Brent — Class of 2010
Toni — Class of 2012
C.J.B.

To my husband, Alan
With special thanks to Alan B.
K.C.

ISBN 0-439-23704-1

12 11 10 9 8 7 6 5 4 3 2 1   1 2 3 4 5 6/0

Printed in the U.S.A.   23

First Scholastic paperback printing, January 2001

CONTENTS

INTRODUCTION

When I grow up I want to be a . . . We all remember making a similar declaration in our own childhood. At the time, it seemed like an eternity until we would be grown up. Now that day is finally here. Graduation Day — a day that marks the beginning of adulthood.

As a graduate dresses in cap and gown and is seated waiting for the commencement ceremony to begin, excitement, exhaustion, and anticipation all combine to create an impatience that will be satisfied only when the diploma is safely in hand.

Later, after the ceremonies are over, someone asks the graduate's opinion of the profoundness of the commencement speech. At that moment, the graduate faces the realization of having missed the entire address! *Hold Fast Your Dreams* is a chance for the recent — and not-so-recent — graduate to relive that special day.

Although our title was taken from a poem of the same name by Louise Driscoll, many of our speakers herein share their dreams, both for themselves and the world. The message is clear: our dreams guide our priorities in life, and thus should be fostered with tender loving care.

Hold Fast Your Dreams
Louise Driscoll

Hold fast your dreams!
Within your heart
Keep one still, secret spot
Where dreams may go,
And sheltered so,
May thrive and grow —
Where doubt and fear are not.
Oh, keep a place apart
Within your heart,
For little dreams to go.

Each of the prominent Americans in this book was invited to deliver a commencement address. These speeches were written with an understanding of the audience's thoughts and feelings at this important moment.

These inspiring commencement speeches were all delivered by members of our society who have earned deserving respect. The selection of speakers in this book was chosen carefully. We made an effort to include a cross-section of outstanding Americans who have a commitment to their cause or field of work. Each of these exceptional individuals has made a significant contribution to our society, yet each has done so in a very different way.

There are twenty speeches in this anthology. Keep

in mind that these speeches were made to an audience; each one was meant to be orated rather than read privately. However, in print, the descriptions, examples, dialogues, questions, and wording create an effective balance of colorful imagery. Instead of these speakers' deliveries, the printed speeches serve as enduring literary examples of the original addresses.

The brief biography preceding the text of each speech is meant to give basic facts and additional insight about the speaker. Woodrow Wilson said, "Eloquence lies in the thought, not in the throat," and so the excellence of the speeches herein does not depend upon their having been spoken. Most of these speeches have been printed in their entirety, and every effort was made to reproduce the speeches as originally delivered.

We hope you will find the rich history and many varying perspectives of this diverse group of speakers interesting. Enjoy these inspiring speeches, each one with its own unique message, and you, too — as we have — will laugh with Cathy Guisewite, cry with Marian Wright Edelman, explore with Robert Ballard, and salute with General Colin Powell.

Carrie J. Boyko   Kimberly Colen

ARTHUR ASHE

Arthur Ashe is the only African–American male tennis player to win both Wimbledon (1975) and the U.S. Open (1968). Born in 1943 in Richmond, Virginia, he became a tennis prodigy and won a scholarship to UCLA. In 1979, a heart attack and bypass surgery forced Ashe to retire. Following a second heart attack in 1983, he contracted AIDS from a blood transfusion. Before his death in 1993, Ashe founded the Association of Tennis Professionals and the African–American Athletic Association. He wrote *A Hard Road to Glory*, tracing the history of African–American athletes. Highlights after his death include the 1996 dedication of a bronze statue in his hometown and the 1997 building of the Arthur Ashe Stadium as the National Tennis Center's main stadium in New York.

ARTHUR ASHE

*Kean College
Union, New Jersey
May 24, 1990*

When I was in college in the sixties, my generation's favorite writer/poet/philosopher was Hermann Hesse — he had a cult following. In his Nobel Prize-winning book, *The Glass Bead Game*, Hesse had a poem entitled "Stages." The first line read, "There is magic in new beginnings." That is what you are doing today: starting over again. Your happiness is deserved.

I welcomed this opportunity to speak solely because I have some views and personal experiences I want to share with you. I believe the subject is very timely, very elusive, very dangerous, and if not confronted will hasten the demise of our nation. If not resolved, then your education will have gone to waste. The issue has two now-familiar titles: multiculturalism and/or cultural diversity.

Both titles refer to efforts and policies that attempt to maintain a group's identity and integrity while simultaneously recognizing and lauding the particularities of individual cultures that make up the groups. Multiculturalism usually refers to nations; cultural diversity usually refers to smaller aggregations like companies, schools, clubs, teams, panels, boards, neighborhoods. Examples abound of na-

3

tions caught up in strife based primarily on an inability to reconcile an appreciation for, and the aspirations of, identifiable but different cultures. The Soviet Union is being rent because Azerbaijanis, Uzbeks, Armenians, Latvians, Lithuanians, and Estonians do not like and never liked domination by ethnic Russians. Canada has a province — Quebec — where forty percent of its voters elected to secede in 1980; to say nothing of its Asian, Indian, West Indian, Aleutian, and Eskimo minorities.

The night before last, I attended a service at the Cathedral of St. John the Divine that Mayor David Dinkins called in response to the ill will created by the Bensonhurst killing and the problems of Korean grocers in black neighborhoods. Something snapped in me, and I felt I had to go because I know what is out there in the world. It is marvelous, it is inspiring, it is illuminating, it is broadening, and there is so much potential for good. I have been fortunate to have played a sport for twenty years that required world travel, but more important to me is that I have friends — real, true, honest-to-goodness friends — everywhere on the globe. But you know something? Before I took my first trip outside America in 1963, I, too, had preconceived ideas about anybody not in the realm of my ordinary experience — and I was wrong just about every time.

In 1968, I was turned down for a visa to play in South Africa solely because I was black. How could people

still feel that way and how could they even rationalize it? Was it really the teachings of the Dutch Reformed Church that blacks were damned by the curse of Ham of the Old Testament and were divinely ordained to be "hewers of wood and porters of water"? Much more recently there were the demands of Asian-Americans at my alma mater, UCLA, and at the University of California at Berkeley that they be let in even if they made up a majority of the freshman classes. You see, the University of California system admits California high school students in the top twelve-and-a-half percent of their classes, but there were many Asian students with GPA's of 4.0 and SAT scores of 1,300 and higher that did not get in. The reason: cultural diversity.

So everybody is mad! Why? Because our national cultural ideal is based on an English model and can be conjured up in mere phrases without explanation. Try these institutions on for size: Harvard, Brooks Brothers, Wall Street, boola-boola, club tie, the royal family, "old boy network," prep school, George Bush, "the Establishment," Founding Fathers.

America is no longer like that, and many minority groups which have traditionally been dealt with paternalistically and patronizingly now demand parity instead of being viewed as an accessory, like a belt or scarf that adds a bit of color to the entire ensemble. There are new entries in our national cultural table of contents, and we can no

longer afford, tolerate, condone, or accept an "Us" versus "Them" mind-set. Our Bill of Rights, in particular the First Amendment, is well on its way toward modern definitions and meaning, in no small measure because some people demand the right to use abusive, racist, sexist, homophobic, and sacrilegious language with impunity.

At that service at St. John's the other night, New York governor Mario Cuomo said it well when he told all listening that bias-related crimes should be especially held in contempt because their victims are singled out because they are different. If we rightfully shudder when reading of such crimes in other countries, we should feel just as chagrined if it happens in Bensonhurst, Howard Beach, Teaneck, or Central Park. You already, no doubt, know that our national workforce will, by the year 2000, be more than two-thirds female and minorities, and I don't mean only African-Americans and Hispanics. What to do?

First, let us not use multiculturalism to stereotype any group. I do not want to be exclusively defined in terms of African-American-ness. I am more than that, and I do not want you to think of me like that no more than Mario Cuomo wants you to think of him as just Italian-American. Do not use our new efforts at multiculturalism to slot or brand anyone. We are all more than what our cultural group may imply in the aggregate.

Second, many white Americans will naturally tend to think of cultural diversity as some equal opportunity

6

issue. Wrong. You will be more affected by it than any other group because you know the least about other national minority groups. I know you, but you do not know me; and I am not Michael Jordan, Bill Cosby, Eddie Murphy, or Sinbad. I have the same hopes as you do, live in a nice house, drive a nice car, play and hope to win the lottery once in a while, send my child to the best school I can.

Let me tell you a true story. I have a friend who is very wealthy, I mean *Forbes* magazine "400" wealthy. I have known the family's children for a long time. Two years ago, one of the family's children applied to one of New York City's preferred private prep schools. The child did not get in. It just so happened that I knew two other children — one African-American and one East Indian — who did, and both were from average families and had to apply for financial aid. Two responses from my wealthy friend disturbed me greatly. The first was the misplaced anger that arose from a belief that wealth equals access on demand. The second was a statement that the two minority five-year-olds got in only because they were minority.

I became quietly enraged. If this person I had known since prepuberty thought and acted ordinarily with such a heightened sense of personal privilege, what could I say about the frightened wage earner who does not really know too many people well outside his or her own insular ethnic group? While no less guilty if he acts in a racist or

sexist manner, at least we understand his own lack of access earlier in his life.

Last year I spoke at Columbia Law School and the one statement I made which engendered fierce but honest and forthright debate was that many of the overwhelmingly white student body at the law school were sitting there because their parents did not have to compete with everyone for access to jobs, housing, education, union cards, promotions, influence, and respect. Society granted to them a side door through which few others could pass. In essence they were the legacies of a caste system with them at the top. That, of course, is changing.

Now, if you are a member of a minority group, there is a limit to the length of time you can posture yourself as a victim. When the NCAA set minimum standards for eligibility for varsity competition at Division I schools, they set the figure at 700 for SAT scores and 2.0 for GPA. Why? Because though it was not written anywhere and no one would say it, the implicit understanding was to set a level "that even black athletes could pass." To the charge that standardized tests are culturally biased, my answer is that maybe they are — I'm no test expert — but at a level of 700, cultural bias wouldn't have much to do with it. You get 400 points for just sitting down and writing your name. And you can take the test as often as you like.

When I was growing up in Richmond, Virginia, in the 1950s, segregation was the law of the state. We were

told things over and over — at school, in church, by our relatives, at scout meetings, at the playgrounds, and by our parents: You are just as good as anybody on the planet; but if you are going to succeed, you will have to be twice as good as anybody else. There was never a thought that we would ever be given preferential treatment. Indeed, the phrase "affirmative action" had not been coined when I was still in public school. I was not allowed to grow up thinking of myself as a victim, and if you look anything like me, neither should you. Just let us all agree on what the rules are, judge fairly, and reward results consistently.

While I understand the motivation behind "minority set-asides," the very notion insults me, even if viewed as a kind of reparation. I have not been a victim of anything — including seventeen years of Virginia's segregation. I have been a survivor, I have overcome, I have persevered, and I have partially succeeded. When you posit yourself as victim, you are actually asking the dominant group to have pity on you. I don't want pity; I demand human parity.

I genuinely feel elated at seeing your faces and knowing how happy you are today, and how relieved your parents are. Some of your parents have postponed dental surgery, taken no vacations, worked extra jobs, and will be in debt for a little while longer. But here they are, so you must have done something right.

In closing, I really do hope you grasp and appreciate

the unrealized potential of this awesome country of ours —
naturally protected by two great oceans on the sides, a
friendly country north of us, a troubled but promising nation just south of the Rio Grande, and an increasing ethnic
diversity that is casting our national character in bold new
forms. Except for Native Americans, we are all immigrants
here, and we must learn to live with one another, among
one another, for one another. It will not be easy, but we
simply have no other alternative.

ROBERT D. BALLARD

Robert D. Ballard has led or participated in nearly 100 deep-sea expeditions, including those to the sunken R.M.S. *Titanic*. Other expeditions led to the discovery of the German battleship *Bismark*, eleven warships from the lost fleet of Guadalcanal, and the exploration of the luxury liner *Lusitania*. In 1997, a landmark expedition to the Mediterranean Sea uncovered ships with cargo spanning over five-hundred years of ancient Roman history. From 1989 to 1991, Dr. Ballard hosted the weekly television program *National Geographic Explorer*, and, in 1990, he founded the JASON Foundation for Education, a program to excite students in science. Dr. Ballard is the founder and current head of the Institute for Exploration (IFE) in Mystic, Connecticut, specializing in deep-ocean archaeology. He was born in 1942 in Wichita, Kansas.

ROBERT D. BALLARD

Worcester Polytechnic Institute
Worcester, Massachusetts
May 23, 1992

Perhaps one of the reasons I have been asked to speak is that I turn fifty in a few weeks yet remain as excited about my future as I did thirty years ago when I was in college preparing to move on to a new phase in my life.

To me, life is a great adventure. A series of journeys within journeys, circles within circles. And like all great journeys, they begin with a dream. When I was growing up, dreams were, and still are, a major part of my life. Everyone should dream and then try to make those dreams come true. For me, my dreams dealt with adventure. My heroes were people like Marco Polo, Captain James Cook, and mythical characters out of Jules Verne's novels. One of my major heroes came from *20,000 Leagues Under the Sea*, with its nuclear submarine *Nautilus* and its great Captain Nemo. My biggest dream was to build a submarine myself and sail around the world underwater — to be Captain Nemo and look out of his magical window to see things no one had ever seen before.

I was lucky with my dreams. My father was an engineer and my older brother a physicist. To them the world was bound by the laws of physics. What a wonderful thing,

13

the laws of physics. Wherever you go in the universe, they apply. If you were to travel to the far reaches of our galaxy and find a planet with intelligent life, those beings may have never heard of communism or capitalism or lawyers or politicians, but they would know the laws of physics. If God wrote any laws to govern us, He certainly wrote these laws. How could anyone be a great explorer like Captain Nemo and not know the laws ruling the planet?

This discovery was a lucky one for me. It meant that the dreams I had were governed by reality. I found that when I tried to live out my dreams, I could. If it obeyed the laws of physics, it was possible. And if it was possible, it was attainable, if I would only take the risk and try.

In an epic journey, after you have a dream, you begin to prepare yourself to pursue that dream. That is what many of you have been doing for the last four years. In my case, my journeys were physical journeys. That is what is so wonderful about what I do. I am able to leave society as we know it and travel to some distant place. Like Jason in search of the Golden Fleece or Ulysses on his odyssey.

When I was growing up, the landmasses of the world were largely explored — and the final frontiers were in space and underwater. Space fascinated me and still does, but the ocean fascinated me even more. I do not know if it was the pull of Nemo or that I grew up in San Diego and the sea was so much a part of my life, literally at my doorstep.

14

I can vividly remember walking along the beautiful sandy beaches of Southern California, searching for treasures washed ashore by the tide. I remember one day finding a Japanese fishing float which had traveled across the broad Pacific Ocean, a journey that must have taken years to complete, finally washing ashore, now waiting to be discovered. I can remember exploring the countless tidal pools at low tide, each a world unto itself. One might have a small school of fish racing around, trying to find a way out. Another an octopus hiding inside a tiny cave, hoping not to be seen. The ever-present sea anemones which closed when I touched them and the small crabs ready to stand their ground and fight to the death should I try to pick them up. I had a friend named Johnny Bickley who went with me on numerous adventures in San Diego Bay, watching the giant manta rays leap into the air, hooking onto a monster who effortlessly broke my line and swam away.

As I was growing up, the sea was always a part of my life. I graduated from walking along the beach and investigating tidal pools to bodysurfing and scuba diving. For some reason, I never had an interest in the top of the sea or, for that matter, the sea itself. It was the land beneath the sea that held my fascination. Perhaps it was my love of mountains. Every time I put on an air tank, I headed straight for the bottom. While in high school I wrote a letter to the Scripps Institution of Oceanography in La Jolla, a place I had visited many times before to see their aquar-

ium or to fish on their pier, if I could sneak out onto it un-detected. A kind scientist at Scripps answered my letter and told me how I could apply for a summer scholarship. I was seventeen years old and the summer of 1959 gave me my first great adventures with the sea. On the first cruise, we were hit by a great storm and limped back to shore. On the second, our ship was almost sunk by a great wave which knocked out the windows in the bridge and exploded the portholes in the galley. It was awesome to watch the waves crash over the ship. I was hooked.

On that cruise, I met another kind scientist who encouraged me to attend the University of California at Santa Barbara, where he was teaching geology. Not know-ing exactly what aspect of the sea I wanted to concentrate on, I majored in all the physical sciences: physics, math, chemistry, and geology. It proved to be my most important decision. This broad-based education in science and tech-nology has made it possible for me to follow the action in my field. I think it is a mistake to narrowly focus your in-terests. The broader your experience, the more you can go with the flow, as time goes on.

My childhood dreams always dealt with the sea. But before I could set out on a marine adventure, I had to pre-pare myself. To carry out my adventures required team-work, leadership, discipline, and a knowledge about the sea, both technical and scientific.

For teamwork I turned to sports, which have always

been an important part of my life — team sports like bas-
ketball to teach me to work with others and individual
sports like tennis to teach me about myself.

Leadership and discipline came from the military,
initially in the Army during the Vietnam era and later in
the Navy, where I remain a commander in the Reserve.
The military put me into major leadership positions long
before I would have had that experience anywhere else.

Your childhood is spent dreaming, your young
adulthood preparing. The moment finally comes when it is
time to venture forth. If your dream is a big one you will
need help, you will need to be part of a team. Initially, you
will follow, but then you will lead. You will never make a
good leader unless you have learned to follow. On those
initial journeys when you are asked to pull your oar while
another leads, learn what it takes to be a team player. Learn
how to get along with others. Learn what loyalty and
honesty are all about. Anyone can get to the top by taking
shortcuts by climbing over the bodies of others. But if you
take that route, your time at the top will be short-lived.

Finally, after working for years to help someone else
live their dream, your turn will come. And when you lead
your team on its first adventure in life, be prepared to fail
initially. For no quest is worth pursuing that does not require you to pass many tests, take numerous risks. Jason
had to tame the wild bulls, Ulysses had to resist the sirens
calling him onto the rocks; Captain Nemo had to face the

giant squid. Every major adventure I have been on over the years has tested me severely with violent storms and lost equipment. My first voyage to find the *Titanic* ended in failure. My first expedition to find the *Bismarck* failed as well. The test you must pass is not whether you fall down or not but whether you can get back up after being knocked down. The journeys you will now begin in life will test you to find how well you prepared your mind, but the hardest tests of all will look to see how determined you are to live your dream, how strong is your heart.

At times it will seem like the storms of life will never end, that the trials you must pass seem to go on forever, but they will end — only after your heart and mind have been tested. I have lived through countless storms at sea. Winds over one hundred miles an hour, swells reaching fifty feet. And when I thought I could not last another minute, the winds dropped off, the seas flattened, and the blue sky appeared and my quest was reached. Be it the *Titanic*, the *Bismarck*, or whatever goal I sought. For me, Neptune would finally say enough is enough. I had passed the test. The sea calmed and Neptune would pull back the veil of watery secrecy and there was what I had been looking for. There was the truth I sought.

Your journey is not over once your goal is reached, your dream fulfilled, the truth attained. The journey is never over until you share what you have learned with others. Then and only then can you begin preparing yourself for

your next adventure. Sharing is the final step, when you give up what you have learned. Giving is not something that may interest you right now, but always remember life is never fulfilled, your journey never over until you take time to give back a portion of what has been given to you.

I congratulate all of you for dreaming dreams and preparing yourself to live those dreams. This is at hand to move on to the next phase. When life knocks you down, which it will, lay there for a second and reflect upon what has happened. Learn from your mistake but then get back up. Do not let anyone stop you from fulfilling your dreams.

KEN BURNS

Ken Burns is the director, producer, co-writer, chief cine-matographer, music director, and executive producer of the landmark television series *The Civil War*. The film won two Emmys, two Grammys, and more than forty other major film and television awards, and earned Burns the 1990 Producer of the Year award from the Producer's Guild. As cofounder of Florentine Films, Burns has produced numerous other docu-mentaries, such as the remarkable biography, *Thomas Jefferson*, and his first film, *Brooklyn Bridge*. Born in Brooklyn, New York, in 1953, he now resides in New Hampshire.

KEN BURNS

Case Western Reserve University
Cleveland, Ohio
May 23, 1993

When I began to prepare for this address, I spoke to a number of friends who had practice with this sort of thing. Their advice and collective wisdom were extremely helpful. One said to avoid clichés like the plague. Another gave the best advice for me (and for you also, graduating students): Be yourself. But one said, "By all means, don't tell them that their future lies ahead of them. That is the worst."

I thought about this and I am now convinced that your future lies *behind* you — in our past, collective and personal. If you do not know where you have been, how can you possibly know where you are going? In the last fifteen years of filmmaking, I have learned many things, but that history is our greatest teacher is perhaps the most important lesson. Now I feel like I am an American possession, like Samoa or Guam. I am possessed by American history.

However, this enthusiasm is by no means shared by all. History, and its valuable advice, continues to recede in importance in schools all over the land. The statistics are now frightening. A majority of graduating high school seniors do not know who Joseph Stalin or Winston Church-

ill were. They do not know of the Declaration of Independence, the Emancipation Proclamation, or the Bill of Rights, which came first and what they signified. And a majority could not tell the correct half century in which the Civil War took place — the most important event in our past.

So, I would like to talk briefly about history. About remembering and forgetting. About things that are coming up in your world that reverberate with our past.

We Americans tend to ignore our past. Perhaps we fear having one and burn it behind us like rocket fuel, always looking forward. But that is a bad thing. The consequences are not just ignorance, or stupidity, or even repeating. It represents the deepest kind of inattention, and it becomes a tear or a gap in who we are as a people.

I think that in each of my own films, and with each film more strongly and completely, I have been seized or possessed by an aspect of American history: something that spoke of the aspirations and struggles and motives of people, in the Brooklyn Bridge, in the Statue of Liberty or the Shakers, something that went to the heart of who we have been to become what we are. And I think that with each film, each story that I have struggled with, my sense has sharpened that a thread runs through all the stories, connects these histories, one to the other.

That thread is the essential American one: the struggle for human freedom—whether of movement and design, of sheer achievement in the Brooklyn Bridge, or of

political freedom in the Statue of Liberty, or of spiritual freedom, freedom of the hand and the heart, in the experiment of the Shakers. I know that this is what has drawn me to the Civil War, for in that war the issue of human freedom came for this country, for our people, to the profoundest and most tragic crux. The historian Shelby Foote has called it the crossroads of our being, but somehow when we crossed over, we forgot where we had been — slavery. I think of what James Symington, a former congressman, said in an interview for our film. Slavery, he said, was merely the horrible statutory expression of a deeper rift between peoples based on race, and this rift is what we struggle still to erase from the hearts and minds of people.

That rift stands at the very center of American history; it is the great challenge to which all our deepest aspirations to freedom must rise. If we forget that, if we forget the great stain of slavery that stands at the heart of our history, we forget who we are, and we make the rift deeper and wider. That is what forgetting is — making the human rift wider.

We are forgetting it even now — on campuses and in suburbs and cities — forgetting that, after all, only 130 years ago, four million Americans were owned by other Americans, that 620,000 Americans died over the issue when our population was a mere thirty million. Two percent died.

We too often tend to think, and this is part of the

forgetting, that those people, those Americans back then, were not the same as us, and thus we cut the thread of identity and responsibility that really binds us to them all the same. But they were very like us. They were health faddists and faith healers, into nature cures, water cures, free love, and women's rights; there was evangelical fervor, spiritual experiment, and religious movement of every kind. But they were worldly realists, too. Two days after the first battle of Bull Run in July of 1861, canny real estate speculators bought up the battlefield to make a second kind of killing as a tourist site. Sound familiar?

Our affinity with those people comes in a blizzard of facts. There were 450 brothels in Washington, D.C., alone during the Civil War: the Union men called a trip to one "going down the line" and spoke of taking "horizonal refreshments." Men like Jay Gould and J. P. Morgan bought inside government knowledge of military situations, then used it to make millions. Philip Armour gave up gold mining to strike it rich packing pork for the Union Army and, what is worse, thereby invented Spam.

I read something several years ago that struck me very deeply, that ultimately convinced me to undertake the most difficult and satisfying experience of my life, producing a film on the Civil War. "From whence shall we expect the approach of danger?" the writer asked. "Shall some trans-Atlantic giant sweep the earth and crush us at a blow?" Then he answered his own question. "Never. All the

armies of Europe and Asia could not by force take a drink from the Ohio River or make a track on the Blue Ridge in the trail of a thousand years. If destruction be our lot we must ourselves be its author and finisher. As a nation of free men we will live forever or die by suicide."

This could have been written today. It was written 150 years ago, well before the Civil War, by a young lawyer from Springfield, Illinois, Abraham Lincoln, who presided over the closest attempt at national suicide Americans ever made. They killed each other over the meaning of freedom in America. And we should remember that.

But the forgetting begins early and continues. Photography came of age during the Civil War, and more than a million images were taken in four years for a public obsessed with seeing, and perhaps also thereby subduing, the shock and carnage they were inflicting upon one another. But the public appetite for war photographs, fantastic during the war, dropped off sharply after Appomattox. Mathew Brady went bankrupt. Thousands of photographs were lost, forgotten, mislaid, or misused. Glass-plate negatives were often sold to gardeners, not for their images but for the glass itself. In the years immediately following Appomattox, the sun slowly burned the filmy image of war from countless greenhouse gardens across the country, as if the memories might be erased. Still later, the glass would be used as lenses in the faceplates of World War I gas masks.

So it comes down to us — whether we know it, or

want to know it, or not. I think we must want to know it, and to know it we must listen to it and see it, not let the image fade. It is not enough to blame it all today on the ultimate glass-plate negative, TV. We must take more responsibility for our memories than that.

What I am trying to say in all of this is that there is a profound connection between remembering and freedom and human attachment. That is what history is to me. Forgetting is the opposite of all that: it is a kind of slavery, and the worst kind of human detachment. It is a profound irony that last month as our President eloquently dedicated a memorial museum to the Holocaust, the very same kind of genocide was taking place in Bosnia, and our government and the world has absolutely no idea what to do about it . . . again.

Which is why we must remember, even when, precisely when, what memory has to tell us is so appalling. It has seemed to me that the meaning of our freedom as Americans is the freedom of memory, which is also a kind of obligation. We must remember that our country was born under the sign that all men were created equal, but we must remember also that the proclamation did not include blacks or women or the poor. We must remember that Abraham Lincoln signed the Emancipation Proclamation, but we must also remember that Lincoln himself thought of recolonizing black Americans to Panama or Africa as late as April of 1861, as the guns opened up at

28

Fort Sumter. We must remember that the Thirteenth and Fourteenth Amendments secured some kind of equality before the law for African-Americans. But we must also remember that equality as a human fact did not come at once, has still to come, and if we do not believe that, we forget.

It is easy, I am sure, during these times of international upheaval and titanic change elsewhere, to smugly convince ourselves that we in this country have somehow triumphantly made it through, that our destiny as a people, a society, a nation is now assured. That, like a perpetual-motion machine, we will go on forever.

Nothing could be more dangerous to our country than this arrogant belief, brought on and amplified as it is by a complete lack of historical awareness amongst us and further reinforced by a modern media cloaked in democratic slogans but dedicated to the most stultifying kind of consumer existence, convincing us to worship gods of commerce and money and selfish advancement above all else.

Today we are in the midst of a new, subtler, perhaps more dangerous Civil War. The first one proved, above all, that a minority view could not secede politically or geographically from this nation.

Now we are poised to fight that war again, and perhaps again and again, this time culturally. The casualties this time will be our sense of common heritage, our sense of humor, our sense of balance, and our sense of cohesion.

The ultimate stakes, though, are just as great as those Abraham Lincoln faced — the union and very survival of our country.

The new movement toward multiculturalism, an admirable and much-needed alternative to the tyranny of the old history of "great white men" and their "great deeds," now begins to suggest a new tyranny, equally if not more destructive than that old form so many of us have struggled long to replace.

What we are seeing is a secession of ideas and identification from the mainstream. In the name of truth, we have created an infinite number of different truths, all pulling in different directions, all oblivious to the old or even a new conception of what the whole could do. "Too much 'pluribus,' not enough 'unum,'" the great historian Arthur Schlesinger says.

Our first Civil War started, Shelby Foote reminds us, because we failed to do what we Americans do best: compromise. "We like to think of ourselves as uncompromising people," he said, "but our genius is for compromise and when that broke down, we started killing each other." The lesson for today is obvious — only tolerance and inclusion can be the answer.

So, I ask those of you graduating today, male or female, black or white or yellow, young or old, straight or gay, Protestant, Catholic, Muslim, Jew, to become soldiers in a new Union Army, an army dedicated to the preserva-

tion of this country's great and true ideals, a vanguard against separatism and disunion.

Two years ago, our world lost a towering historical and literary figure, the novelist Isaac Bashevis Singer. For decades he wrote, almost sang, about God and myth and punishment, fate and sexuality and family, and history.

He wrote in Yiddish, a marvelous, expressive language, sad and happy all at the same time, sometimes maddeningly all knowing and yet resigned to God's seemingly capricious will. It is also a language without a country, a dying language in a world more often interested in the extermination or isolation of its troubled, long-suffering speakers. Singer, first writing in this country in the pages of the *Jewish Daily Forward*, almost single-handedly helped to keep Yiddish alive. Now our own wonderfully mongrel American language is punctuated with dozens of Yiddish words and phrases, parables and wisdom. And so many of these words are perfect onomatopoeias of disgust and humor, description and hubris. If you have ever met a schmuck, you know what I am talking about.

Toward the end of his long and prolific life, he expressed wonder at why so many of his books, written in this obscure and, some said, useless language, would be so widely translated in something like fifty-six countries all around the world. Why, for example, he wondered, would the Japanese care about his simple stories of life in the shtetels of Eastern Europe a thousand years ago? "Unless,"

Singer paused, answering his own question elegantly and magnificently, "unless these stories spoke of the kinship of the soul"; that which connects all of us together, that which we all share as part of the life of this planet.

Kinship of the soul . . .

I have had my own wonderful brush with "kinship of the soul" the last few years as I attempt to digest the reaction and impact of the Civil War series, both serious and frivolous, on our country. Nowhere is the profundity of response more pronounced than in the wonderful, touching, and expressive letters I have received. To my surprise and delight, the eloquence of the common man that we had worked so hard to put in our film came through in thousands of new letters from Americans who were supposed to be completely numbed by television and a postmodern age that had lulled them to blissful, ignorant sleep. Let me read you just one example, from Gregory Alan Gross. His letter speaks to my own remarks and says it better than a hundred commencement addresses:

> Dear Sir:
>
> Again, I am watching *The Civil War* — enthralled, inspired, heartbroken. So much to think about, so much to feel:
>
> The eloquence of ordinary people resounds. It humbles me.
>
> Such dignity in the archival faces of

my people, who were enslaved but who never surrendered their souls to slavery.

Then I hear the Southerners who not only kept my ancestors in bondage, but fought to the death to do so. And I hate them for that.

Then the choir in the film sings: "Do you . . . do you . . . want your freedom?" A good question, for we are not yet truly free, none of us.

To achieve that, white America must abandon its racial conceits — and I must abandon my hate. They must change, and I must forgive, for us both to be free.

Lincoln was right. "Malice toward none, charity for all."

So at the end, I wonder. Does my white counterpart, hearing that choir, realize that that final question is meant for both of us?

"Do you . . . do you . . . want your freedom?"

I know what my answer is. I will wait for him.

So what do we make of all this? Let me speak directly to the graduating class. Watch out, here comes the advice.

As you pursue your goals in life, that is your future, pursue your past. Let it be your guide. Insist on having a past, and then you will have a future.

Stay involved with your school. It needs your attention as well as your money to keep perpetually moving.

Do not descend too deeply into specialism in your work. Educate all of your parts. You will be healthier, I promise.

Do not confuse success with excellence. The poet Robert Penn Warren once told me that "careerism is death."

Travel. Do not get stuck in one place. Visit Appomattox, where our country really came together. And whatever you do, please walk over the Brooklyn Bridge.

Give up addictions of all kinds. For example, try brushing your teeth tonight with the other hand. Try even remembering what I just asked you.

Insist on heroes. Insist on heroes. And then be one.

Read. The book is still the greatest man-made machine of all — not the car, not the TV, I promise you.

By all means, write: write letters. Keep journals. Besides your children, there is no surer way of achieving immortality. Write: send messages. There is nothing more incredible than being a witness to history.

Serve your country. Insist that we fight the right wars. Convince your government that the real threat comes from within, just as Abraham Lincoln said. Governments always forget that. Insist that we support science and

the arts, especially the arts. They have absolutely nothing to do with the defense of the country — they only make our country worth defending.

Finally, let me leave you with a message from the late journalist Eric Sevareid:

> Man himself is a precarious balance between love and hate, generosity and selfishness, peaceableness and aggressiveness. He is not perfectible but he is improvable, and nothing in his history or his nature obliges one to abandon belief in him. He may indeed be forever "trapped between Earth and a glimpse of heaven," but he will hold to that glimpse, as we must.

JIMMY CARTER

Former U.S. President Jimmy Carter now holds a professorship at Emory University and runs the Carter Center, which
addresses national and international issues of public policy.
Mr. Carter champions human rights all over the world, while
actively involving himself in Habitat for Humanity and his
local church. The author of fourteen books, James Earl
Carter, Jr. was born in 1924 in Plains, Georgia, and grew up
in the nearby community of Archery. Following his education, Mr. Carter joined the Navy and worked on the development of the nuclear submarine program. He later took
over his father's farm supply business and became interested
in community affairs in Plains, which led to his career in state
and national politics.

JIMMY CARTER

Rice University
Houston, Texas
May 8, 1993

I have just finished my eleventh year as a distinguished professor at Emory University, which I have enjoyed. On a few occasions I have been introduced by my boss, Jim Laney, the president of Emory, who exalts a professorship at Emory perhaps above what it should be. His standard introduction, at least to a new crowd, is, "Ladies and gentlemen, I want to introduce to you former president Jimmy Carter, the only man who has ever used the presidency as a stepping-stone to greater things." On the other hand, I was introduced by one of my fellows at the Carter Center recently, on the twenty-fifth anniversary of the Peace Corps. My mother was an active Peace Corps member in India, and there was a very distinguished crowd there, and this fellow, Robert Pastor, said, "I want to introduce to you President Jimmy Carter, a man without whom the Carter Center would not have its first name." So you can see where there is a whole range of introductions I have been subjected to.

I have had a good life since I left the White House. I am not going to dwell on that too much. We make our living writing books. My wife's only request was to an-

39

nounce to you that our books are still on sale. I am going to be fairly brief this morning and talk to you from my heart, not from a text, about my thoughts as a former governor, as a former president, as someone who knows the world fairly well from that unique perspective, and try to give you in an informal fashion some thoughts that you might consider.

Almost everyone here, perhaps everyone, has been born in this century, within the last ninety-three years. And we know the dynamic change that has taken place in society during that period of time. There are three basic elements that have brought about the change: the aftermath of the Industrial Revolution, rapidly increasing literacy, and also, of course, the urbanization of societies, both in this country and around the world. These have stimulated new thoughts, new ideas, new actions, new interrelationships among people. You might say, well, that is a blessing. But the fact is that this century, far beyond any other in history, has been burdened with tragedy — the unanticipated, deliberate murder of people by their own governments. Deaths on the battlefield have far exceeded all [those in] the previous time that is recorded for us to know. World War I and World War II, in which my father and I were involved, cost 43 million lives. Deaths directly resulting from persecution by Adolf Hitler and by Stalin amounted to more than 30 million deliberate murders of people within their own countries. This is perhaps even

40

exceeded in China. We do not know. And those kinds of afflictions have continued in this century.

At the Carter Center, one of our duties is to monitor — every day — all the conflicts in the world. You might be interested in knowing there are now 112 that we monitor. Thirty-two of these are major wars. A major war by our definition is one within which more than 1,000 people are killed on the battlefield each year. And in modern-day wars, there are almost ten civilians killed for each soldier killed.

There have never been in history as many ongoing major wars as there are right now. Unfortunately, almost all these are civil wars. With the exception of Yugoslavia, which was one country, all of these wars are within a single country. Horrendous in scope, more than a million people died in Ethiopia in that thirty-year war. Two hundred thousand or more people died in Sudan in just one year recently.

The problem is that the United Nations is not authorized to go into these countries except under rare circumstances, because it is not proper for a UN official to speak to a revolutionary group trying to change or overthrow a government that is a member of the UN. So this is a symbol of what is going on. We do not know about most of these wars in the United States.

We know about a Somalia once it comes to the forefront on CNN and in other media. We know about Bosnia now, but the others escape our awareness. And the

ethnic cleansing in Bosnia is not a unique thing on earth. Racial, religious, ethnic differences still cause tremendous suffering, deliberately perpetrated by one human being against another. This is quite understandable by the average person. Despite the end of the Cold War with the advent of Gorbachev and so forth, a recent poll — one that was taken two weeks ago, as a matter of fact — showed that fifty-eight percent of the American people believe that the world is more dangerous now than it was five years ago.

That is the sad side of it. What can be done about it? By me, by our country, by you as graduates and by a great university? I am going to leave here in a few minutes, as soon as my speech is over, in order to get to Paraguay before midnight, because some of our tasks at the Carter Center are to try to bring an end to conflict or to prevent conflicts, and to bring democracy and peace and human rights to countries through free elections. Quite often, and increasingly, those at war, or those who are filled with hatred or division, are willing to resolve their differences through elections. As a politician, I know that politics is a science of self-delusion. If you want to run for mayor, or run for governor, you are convinced that if the election is honest and if people know you and know all these other characters, they will surely vote for you. Right? So they invite us to come in, and that is what I am going to do in Paraguay the next few days.

At the end of the Cold War, the United States of

America — more than any other time, even immediately after the Second World War — has become the world's superpower, responsible in an increasing way to shape attitudes among the world's human beings. We cannot be the world's policemen. That is not what I am talking about. But the economic, political, military, and cultural influences of the United States permeate the world.

What characteristics are there that our country should put forward to correct some of the problems that I outlined very briefly about the twentieth century? What are some of the characteristics of a nation? A commitment to peace, to democracy or freedom, to human rights, to environmental quality, and to sharing our wealth with others? How our country will measure up to those very high standards it is hard for us yet to say. What are the great resources we have in addition to arable land and good streams and warm oceans and friendly neighbors and great mineral deposits and so forth?

One of the greatest treasures that we have is here at Rice University. We are challenged in economic terms, trade terms, productivity terms, by other countries: Europe, Japan, and so forth. No other nation can challenge us in the quality of our university system. We have now 200,000 foreign students in American universities, most at the graduate level. The largest number, by the way, is from China: 75,000. What is the impact of this repository of learning, teaching, study, and analysis in the rest of the

world? It is hunger for knowledge and assistance and advice.

Recently I was in Africa, in Nairobi, Kenya, as a matter of fact, and I was at a table with eight people — ministers from African countries — and I asked them, "What do American universities mean to you?" I had a little hand-held recorder, and I handed it around and said, "Each one of you make a very brief statement." I recorded those. Let me just read what some of them said. This one is from the foreign minister of the Seychelles. He said, "American universities are rarely relevant." The minister of agriculture from Uganda, who happened to be a woman, said, "What is known is not shared with those needing to know. Information is just exchanged among academics who never witness hunger or have personal knowledge of torture or see a denuded landscape. How many university presidents have been to a village where river blindness is prevalent, or Guinea worm or constant plague?" The finance minister from Ghana said, "We know that almost everything is connected — health, nutrition, environmental quality, political stability, human rights. Some leading educators understand this, but the information is not even shared with our government ministers, whose decisions control our lives." A minister from Zambia said universities should be where the highest ideals are preserved, but they exhibit little interest in our problems. My favorite was one from a Nigerian who said, "One action is better than a hundred conferences."

This was a sobering thing. On the way back, I asked

an American scientist — who perhaps feels affected by lives all over the world as much as anyone — what he thought about it, and he said, "In the education of my own children I would want them to acquire three things. First of all, an inquisitive mind — always exploring new ideas, questioning old ones, not afraid to challenge status quo. Second, I would want them to know that there is a cause-and-effect relationship. This is not a fatalistic world inhabited by people whose suffering is inevitable and whose problems cannot be solved. And third, I would want them to know that they are world citizens. Their lives are inextricably tied to those in other nations. I would want them eager to learn foreign languages, forced to, if necessary."

Universities are a resource that is rarely tapped. And the initiative has to come from within universities. This is one of the best universities of all, and I would hope that there would be an exploration of what can be done on a global basis, and certainly within our country. How can we relate to people who are suffering in Somalia and Haiti? How can we prevent the catastrophes that permeate the world? I know about discrimination. I grew up in the South. I was embarrassed, at least as an adult, by racial discrimination. I have been in Sudan lately; I will be there again in two months. It is a country that is torn apart by religious discrimination. A central fundamentalist Muslim government is oppressing, in my opinion, those of other religions in the same country.

45

But I tell you that the greatest discrimination on earth today, including in our own country, is discrimination by the rich against the poor. Who are the rich? I am not talking about definitions based on bank accounts. But I would say that everyone here is rich. We do not deliberately discriminate. A rich person is someone with a home and a modicum of education and a chance, at least, for a job. A rich person is one who believes that if he makes a decision it will have some effect, at least, in his own life, and who believes that the police and the judges are on his side. Those are the rich people.

We have neighbors who have none of those advantages — neighbors we rarely know. I teach Sunday school every Sunday morning when I am in Plains, and I know that our churches — there are 10,000 of them in Atlanta, plus the synagogues and mosques — usually are encapsulated in ivory towers where we meet people just like us. We admire each other, we brag about our religious commitment, and rarely know the people next door who exemplify the kind of suffering for which we pledge to commit a major part of our lives.

There are really two Americas. One rich America. One poor America. There are two Atlantas, two Houstons — rarely do they know each other.

What can we do about it? Nobody can force us to reach out and say, "I care for you." In closing, let me just give you three personal examples of people who work in-

timately with the Carter Center and with me and Rosalynn. One of them still teaches in Texas. His name is Norman Borlaug, and he comes from a little town in Iowa. He got a good education, like you are getting. He is a plant geneticist. He went to Mexico; he spent most of his life there breeding new kinds of corn and rice. In the early 1970s he went to India and Pakistan, where massive hunger and starvation were taking place, and almost single-handedly brought about what is known as a Green Revolution. He won the Nobel Peace Prize for it. He works with us now. With him and others at the Carter Center, we now have 150,000 small farmers in Africa rapidly increasing their production of basic food grains — wheat, millet, sorghum, and corn, which they call maize. Dr. Borlaug goes out on the farms — he is now almost ninety years old — where they worship him, almost, as someone who can change their lives. He has helped to develop a new kind of corn, a white corn, that has all the amino acids in it, which other corn has never had at any time in history. Now, when a woman takes her baby off her breast milk and puts that baby on cornmeal mush or grits, that baby can have adequate nutrition. This is one man, working almost alone, with a good education and dedicated to his own career but at the same time caring for the rest of the world.

Another person I will mention is Dr. William Foege, who has been the director of our center. Dr. Foege comes from a missionary family. He worked in West Africa

as a missionary. He is a medical doctor, perhaps preeminent in preventive health care. Dr. Foege was head of the Centers for Disease Control in Atlanta for ten years. He orchestrated the eradication of smallpox, the only disease ever eradicated, and now Dr. Foege is in charge of a task force on child survival at the Carter Center. Eight years ago the World Health Organization, UNICEF, and others came to us and said, "We are not able to immunize the world's children. We are all in competition with each other." WHO and UNICEF did not speak to each other, and they would go into a country at different times. They only had twenty percent of the world's children immunized against polio, measles, diphtheria, tetanus, and whooping cough. They asked Dr. Foege to put together a team, which he did. In five years, with no increase in funding, no increase in personnel, we were able to increase from twenty percent to eighty percent the number of the world's children immunized. One man, good education, dedicated, taking care of his own career, but reaching out to others.

Another one is named Millard Fuller. Millard Fuller was a successful law school graduate at the University of Alabama. He made a lot of money while he was still a student selling cookbooks and also delivering flowers or cakes on birthdays of students — at the University of Alabama, for a fee. Then he made more than a million dollars in a few years after graduation. But his wife told him, "If all you want to do is to make money, I'm leaving." She left,

went to New York with the three kids. Millard followed her up to New York; they rode around in a taxicab. He finally said, "I'll give away all my money if you won't leave me." He did. He gave away every cent he had. He came down about nine miles from Plains, Georgia, and began to build homes for poor people in need. Then he spent three years in Zaire and came back and organized Habitat for Humanity.

Habitat was a simple idea for volunteers to go out and work side by side with the poorest families in our country. Today, it has chapters in almost forty foreign nations. Rosalynn and I and other volunteers build homes for those poor people, working side by side with them. There is no charity involved. The family has to put in at least 500 hours on its own house, one fourth of the total construction time of 2,000 hours. And they have to pay full price for the house, but they receive interest-free loans. The Bible says when you lend money to a poor person, you do not charge interest.

Last month, we finished the 20,000th house in Americus, Georgia. It took us sixteen years to build the first 20,000. We will pass the 30,000 mark next year, as Habitat grows rapidly. But the point is, this is one man, a lawyer, not a preacher, not a very good carpenter, who took advantge of his education, his background, his opportunities and followed his own career but cared for others.

That is the kind of thing we can do individually,

and that individual contribution can feed back through our universities and through our U.S. government and our great nation to bring about a world that can be filled with peace and with freedom and can protect human rights and can have a quality environment and within which we can share, and the sharing is not a sacrifice.

Those of us who build a Habitat house feel a lot better than if we had stayed at home. And the families receive the home — the first decent house they have ever had — with a lot of tears, a lot of songs, a lot of prayers, a lot of thanks. We are just as thankful as the homeowners are.

Well, I have come to the end of my talk. What is the message here? I would say youth and vigor and idealism and knowledge and sharing, and I think, above all, freedom.

When you are at your age and have emerged from college with an expanded mind and expanded heart to learn more about other people and more about God's world, it is the best time to say, "What will I do with my life? How can I be successful?" and more important, "What is success?"

This was a question asked by the early Christians of Paul: "What are the permanent things in life?" And I am sure they had the same image in their mind as you have. A good house, good transportation, security in one's old age. And Paul said, "The permanent things are the things that you cannot see." They were in a quandary about what he

meant. He was talking about justice and truth and sharing and service and compassion, and if you will excuse the expression, love.

So as we embark on the rest of our lives, either as graduates or just the next day, perhaps we could keep in mind how the world has been changing, how it might change in the future, how our influence through an educational institution and through a great nation can affect the opportunities that we have. Young people can change the world. My three sons came along quite early in mine and Rosalynn's married life, during the late sixties, and I would say they and their college classmates changed this nation. They got us out of Vietnam, brought about civil rights laws, and organized Earth Day. These were great, exhilarating times. Our government was very reluctant to change, as you know. Amy came along fifteen years later. Rosalynn and I had a fourteen-year argument that I finally won, and Amy arrived. She is our second generation; she is still in college. It is not that there is not the dynamism and the quizzical nature and the commitment in college students now as there was then. I am not advocating it, but Amy, who is one of the most timid people I have ever met, has been arrested four times because she believes that there should be an end to apartheid. She was concerned about some of the politics of our government. She was put on trial in Massachusetts for protesting, as a matter of fact, which interrupted a whole year of her studies. She was

found innocent by a strange Massachusetts law. This law said Amy and twelve others did commit a serious offense, but Massachusetts law states that if the offense that you commit is designed to prevent a greater crime, then you are innocent. So Amy was found innocent, and she pointed out that all the jurors were more than thirty years old.

So you see, within us individually there should be a searching, a reaching, a grasping, or a quizzical attitude, a questioning of society, a questioning of ourselves. How can I rejuvenate myself and apply in my life the true measures of success? Excellence comes from a repository that doesn't change, like the last eighty years here at Rice. How do we take that excellence in our life and a vision of America and a troubled world, and with but one life — my own — make it great? That is the challenge for us all. Certainly including me. When I think about Norman Borlaug, and Millard Fuller, and Bill Foege, and many others like them, I see that the limitations on my life should be removed and the freedom that comes with a commitment to be free can give us a life full of joy, peace, and true success. That is what I wish for you.

BEN COHEN

After dropping out of two colleges and holding a string of jobs, Ben Cohen and his childhood pal, Jerry Greenfield, opened the first Ben & Jerry's Homemade Ice Cream parlor in 1978. This shop soon earned a reputation for rich, exotic flavors of ice cream. Their community-oriented approach to business and their unique commitment to social responsibility has been recognized with national awards. Today this company boasts sales in excess of $237 million. Born in Brooklyn, New York, in 1951, Cohen grew up in Merrick, Long Island, making his own varieties of ice cream as a child and working as an ice cream man in high school.

BEN COHEN

Vassar College
Poughkeepsie, New York
May 23, 1993

I want to tell you a little about how I got to be where I am today, standing here before you. Jerry and I met in gym class in junior high school. We were the two slowest, fattest kids in the class. The whole class would be running around the track, and in back were me and Jerry. You make pretty close friends with whomever you can find back there.

Then I went on to a college career. I dropped out of all those colleges I went to, and I've been receiving my college degrees in the honorarial fashion. You know, the first time they invited me to speak at a college graduation, they gave me an honorary doctorate, and I walked off with this thing that says, "Doctor of Commercial Sciences." And it says you're entitled to all the rights and privileges of all the rest of the doctors of commercial sciences, but I've never been able to find another doctor of commercial sciences. I got a D.C.S.; what have you got, man? Well, Vassar don't play games; they ain't giving me nothing for this.

It was wonderful to hear this is the age of Ben & Jerry's. That is the first time that has been said, but hopefully this will go forth.

I want to start off with an old Indian saying:

When you were born,
you cried and the world rejoiced.
Live your life in such a way that when you die
the world cries and you rejoice.

So, the content of my talk today is "What's going on? How did that happen? And how are we going to get ourselves out of this mess?" I have a literary reference here to start off. Just as Dickens wrote back in 18-whatever, "It is the best of times. It is the worst of times."

The enemy has collapsed. The nuclear threat has been minimized. Our own country's economy is in a shambles. There are riots in the streets. We can produce enough food to feed everyone on earth and yet 30,000 children a day are dying of starvation and preventable disease. The ability to communicate around the world virtually instantaneously brings us closer together and yet neighboring countries are at war. The very rich in our country continue to get richer while the number and percentage of people living in poverty continues to swell. And even the middle class is lagging behind. One out of every four American babies is born into poverty.

We have developed the computer, the best instructional aid the world has ever seen, while illiteracy and school dropout rates continue to soar. We have made an incredible number of technological advances, but the vast majority have been directed toward developing new meth-

ods of killing people for the military. The concentration of our nation's resources into the military-industrial complex has allowed our country to become the largest exporter of arms in the world. The Cold War has been over for a few years now, but the military budget remains about the same as it was during the Cold War years. It is not needed to defend ourselves against the Soviet Union. Fully half of that military budget is spent to defend Western Europe from a Warsaw Pact that no longer exists. The military budget has become a jobs bill. A shortsighted and dead-end one at that, because when we use our nation's capital and our nation's resources in order to build weapons, it is a dead end. The weapons are stored, hopefully never to be used. Whereas, if we could redirect that money into building our physical and human asset base, we could grow our economy and work with those assets. We now have that money to spend on those physical and human capital bases. And on top of that, every 3 billion dollars that we transfer from the military sector to the civilian sector creates 12,000 more jobs. According to the Center for Defense Information, we could reduce our military budget by 78 billion dollars per year and still have the strongest military force in the world.

As Einstein told us, it is impossible to simultaneously prevent and prepare for war. We have billions of dollars for the Gulf War, for space exploration, for road construction for the military, and the S&L bailout, and virtually no money to provide for basic human needs, eco-

nomic development, or education for people living in poverty. What is puzzling me is not that L.A. burned, but that the rest of the cities are not burning as well.

Martin Luther King talked about this situation. He said that "the means by which we live have outdistanced the ends for which we live. We have learned the secret of the atom but have forgotten the Sermon on the Mount. Our technical mastery has outstripped our spiritual capacity. We have guided missiles and misguided men." We are ruled by men with an uncontrollable urge to blow things up. BABOOM! We have enough bombs to blow up every major city on earth twenty times over. BABOOM! The world is participating in a nuclear test ban, but we decide that we need to start testing nuclear weapons again. BA-BOOM!

In the little state of Vermont, we have rock outcroppings along the sides of the interstate. Last summer they started blowing those things up. People started saying, "What's going on here? There's no problem with these rock outcroppings." It turns out there was federal money and it was free, and you know, let's blow up our rocks. Well, people started protesting. They started sitting on top of the rocks to save them. Finally they stopped blowing up the rocks, and then as soon as spring rolled around this year they came back with a vengeance. BABOOM! No more rocks in Vermont.

We elected a new president. Then we refused to

allow him to carry out his economic and spiritual program due to politics. And then when we ask him to do the rest of the stuff that he has promised to do, he is not able to do it because it all depends on an economic program. This is not, despite what it appears to be, a democracy that we're living in today. This is not the rule of the people, by the people, for the people. An increasingly small percentage of the people vote. And it is not really surprising. I mean, look at the choices that we give them. For somebody living in poverty today, you have a chance of voting for a government which decides that instead of securing your neighborhoods and creating a world for your children whereby they can once again say "*when* I grow up" instead of "*if* I grow up," we will spend your money on exploring outer space and creating more military madness.

With the money the U.S. spends on weapons we could feed and care for every one of those 30,000 children around the world who are dying every day of preventable disease. And we can eliminate the poverty that afflicts one out of four American children as well. There will never be peace, there will never be security in our country or in our world, as long as we use the tool of capitalism to take necessities from the many to give luxuries to the few.

What is going on here? What is going on is capitalism run amuck. A heartless, soulless, Frankensteinian monster on a rampage. We are destroying ourselves. The monster of capitalism is devouring our democracy. I think a lot of

this is due to the phenomenon of the compartmentaliza-
tion of our lives. We have become disintegrated. Our lives
are split up so that when we go to business, when we go to
work, our task there is to earn a living. Our task there is
solely economic. We're told to leave our values at the door.
We go to our house of worship and it is there that we do
our spiritual work. But, of course, the irony is that it is impossible to actualize that spiritual work except when we're
outside those houses of worship. We deal with the social
needs of our communities when somebody knocks on the
door and we give them a few bucks or when we do volun-
teer work at home in our spare time.

Business has created itself, has defined itself in order
to say that the only legitimate role of business is to maxi-
mize profits. What we're learning at Ben & Jerry's is that
you only get what you measure. You see that in your own
personal life. If you're on a diet and you want to lose weight
you've got to constantly measure your weight. You've got
to constantly weigh yourself. That keeps you focused on
what you are trying to do. It keeps you thinking about it.
In business the only way we measure success is by how
much money is left over at the end of the year. That is the
only thing that business is measured on. That is the only
thing that business focuses on. It is the only thing business
concentrates on. That is kind of sad because business has
now become the most powerful force in the world.

It did not used to be that way. Originally the most

powerful force in the world was religion, and then, as time went by, the most powerful force in the world came to be nation-states. Today it is business. You can see this echoed in the size of the buildings in our major cities. You can see that the first one was a religious building. Then later the biggest, most ornate building came to be a governmental building. Today, the biggest, most ornate buildings are commercial. So business is now the most powerful force in the world, but it does not even have the pretext of being concerned about our social or spiritual life.

Business tends to act in a win/lose fashion. It is business versus the environment. Business acts in the legislative and political arenas in order to carry on that fight. It is business versus its employees, and that is what is going on with union and management. It is business versus consumers, and that is what brings about consumer activism, the need for consumer activism, and Ralph Nader's groups.

Business cares only about its narrow self-interest. That is the issue we need to attack. Because it is the most powerful influence in the whole world and it influences every part of our lives. The big, powerful corporations are the ones that the individuals and the smaller businesses are learning from. What we learn from them is: Don't be concerned about people, ignore human suffering, pollute and break the law if you've got enough money to pay for enough lawyers. This is a perversion of capitalism, and it gets worse as business becomes bigger and more imper-

sonal with conglomerates and multinationals. This is a new phenomenon because this is not how it used to be. It is new since we have concentrated wealth and power into the hands of this small number of multinational businesses. The irony here is that the people who run those large corporations are caring people who have the same social concerns that you and I have.

The last part of this talk is about how we get out of this mess. The solution is to reintegrate, to view things in a more holistic manner, to integrate our social, spiritual, and economic work together.

When Ben & Jerry's started getting larger, Jerry and I kind of looked at ourselves and said, "Oh, man! This isn't good anymore. We're not scooping ice cream anymore, we're not making ice cream anymore. We are businesspeople. We are writing memos, hiring people, firing people, balancing the books." This was not what we had in mind. So we started thinking about the definition of business. Most people will define business as an entity that produces a product or provides a service.

At Ben & Jerry's we define it differently. We say that business is a combination of organized human energy plus money, which equals power. The sad part is that when we are organized in that most effective fashion, we are told to leave our values at the door. This is because, except for maximizing profit, businesses tend to be valueless. You can understand the power of business if you think about this

example: If we were to all go home tonight *as individuals* and attempt to solve a particular social problem, we would be much less effective than if we were to all do it together, *organized* as a business working on that same problem.

It becomes more and more clear to us at Ben & Jerry's that there is a spiritual aspect to business, just as there is to the lives of individuals. And just because the idea that the good you do comes back to you is written in the Bible and not in some business textbook does not mean that it is any less valid. We are all interconnected, and as we help others we cannot help but to help ourselves.

So we realized this at Ben & Jerry's, and we said, "Okay. So why is it that these good people get together and then the organization does not act upon social values?" We realized that it is because of how we measure ourselves, that the sole measure for business success is how much money is left over at the end of the year — the bottom line. So, what we said at Ben & Jerry's is that if the measure of success is what determines how the organization functions, and we want to change the way the organization functions, why don't we just change our measure of success, which is what we did.

Now instead of the amount of money being left over at the end of the year being our sole measure of success, we have a two-part bottom line, and we also measure how much we have helped to improve the quality of life in our communities. We measure both halves of our bottom

line. In our annual report you will see a social audit right next to our financial audit. When we evaluate our employees and our managers, they are evaluated on how much they have helped to bring more money to the organization and how much they have worked to improve the quality of life in the community.

At first, when we started doing this, our managers came back to us and said, "It sounds like a nice idea, guys, but we can't do this. Every time we start using company resources to improve the quality of life in the community, that takes away company resources we can use to increase profits, and vice versa." We thought about this for a while, and we finally realized that the answer to the dilemma was to choose those courses of action that have a positive effect on both sides of the bottom line. That is what we have been doing for the last five, six, or seven years at Ben & Jerry's.

The interesting thing about it is that it is a paradigm shift. It is hard to get your head to think that way because you are so used to saying that we do our social good works over there and make our money over here. But we have been able to combine the two.

One example is our Peace Pops. We were going to come out with a chocolate-covered pop on a stick. We realized that there was going to be this package and there was going to be millions of them going out. Instead of talking about how great this product is on the package, we could

instead talk about the need to redirect money out of the military and into social and environmental needs. So we started using the package for that.

Once you do one, the others come quickly. We found a company that makes brownies. It is run by a religious community that teaches homeless people how to become bakers and provides them with housing. Just by deciding to consciously source our brownies from that company, we are able to make a positive impact on the community and make money at the same time.

This is a paradigm shift, and it meets with incredible resistance. Schopenhauer said that "All truth goes through three stages: First, it is ridiculed; second, it is violently opposed; third, it is accepted as being self-evident." Rosabeth Moss Kanter, writing in the *Harvard Business Review*, said that "Money should never be separated from mission. It is an instrument, not an end. Detached from values, it may be the root of all evil. Linked effectively to social purpose, it can be the root of opportunity."

It becomes more and more clear to us at Ben & Jerry's that our success is testament to the power of the human spirit when people are joined together in working for the common good.

Martin Luther King said that

> The stability of the large world house, which
> is ours, will involve a revolution of values

to accompany the scientific and freedom revolutions engulfing the earth. We must rapidly shift from a thing-oriented society to a person-oriented society. When machines and computers, profit motives, and property rights are considered more important than people, the giant triplets of racism, material-ism, and militarism are incapable of being conquered. A civilization can flounder as read-ily in the face of moral and spiritual bank-ruptcy as it can through financial bankruptcy.

I am going to get into the grand finale now: a bar-rage of pithy quotes and stories, not unlike the earth-shattering display of fireworks on the Fourth of July. I would like to begin with a quote from our former vice president Dan Quayle: "What a waste it is to lose one's mind." But I don't mean it the way he meant it. I mean it the way he said it. Do not just become a cog in the system of economic oppression, which is what our society is about today.

Tracy Chapman said, "Don't give or sell your soul away. Hunger for the taste of justice. Hunger for the taste of freedom. All that you've got is your soul."

And from Lily Tomlin, "The trouble with being in the rat race is that even if you win, you'll still be a rat."

And this is it. This is the very, very end here. It is an

ancient Eastern story of the man who was granted permission to see both heaven and hell while he was still alive. He made a deal with this angel. He decides to see hell first. He goes down with the angel and they open up this big door and they look inside. It is a beautiful banquet hall, and down the middle is this long banquet table with people seated on either side, with every imaginable delicacy in bowls and platters all along the whole table. He is puzzled to see that the people there are wailing and crying and they are in misery. He looks a little closer and he sees that the handles on their eating utensils are so long that it is impossible to get the food into their mouths. Depressed and with a heavy heart, he asked to go see heaven.

They go over, they open up a door that looks pretty much the same, they open it up, and it is just about the same scene — a huge banquet hall, table down the middle, people seated on both sides. The table is laden with every imaginable delicacy. The greatest food you have ever seen in your life. He looks and sees that the handles on the utensils are also really, really long. But these people are laughing and singing and rejoicing. He looks closer and sees that the people in heaven, instead of trying to feed only themselves, were feeding each other.

MARIAN WRIGHT EDELMAN

Marian Wright Edelman is the founder and president of the Children's Defense Fund, an organization with a strong national voice for children and families whose mission is to educate the nation about the needs of children. Edelman began her career in the mid-sixties when, as the first black woman admitted to the Mississippi Bar, she directed the NAACP Legal Defense and Educational Fund office in Jackson. Born in 1939 in Bennettsville, South Carolina, her entire career has involved advocating for disadvantaged Americans. Her prestigious awards include a MacArthur Foundation Prize Fellow and the Albert Schweitzer Humanitarian Prize. She is the author of several books including the popular, *The Measure of Our Success: A Letter to My Children and Yours* and *Lanterns: A Memoir of Mentors*.

MARIAN WRIGHT EDELMAN

Washington University
St. Louis, Missouri
May 15, 1992

When I was growing up in my little rural Southern segregated town, service was as essential a part of my upbringing as eating and sleeping. Caring black adults were buffers against the external world that told me I, a black girl, was not important. But I did not believe it because my parents said it wasn't so. My teachers and preachers said it wasn't so. So the childhood message I internalized was that as a child of God, no man or woman could look down on me and I could look down on no man or woman.

I could not play in segregated public playgrounds or sit at drugstore lunch counters, so Daddy, a Baptist minister, built a playground and canteen behind our church. Whenever he and my mother saw a need, they tried to respond. There were no black homes for the aged in my rural segregated town, so my parents began one across the street, and all of our family had to help out. I sure did not like it a whole lot at the time, but that is how I learned that it was my responsibility to take care of elderly family members and neighbors, and that everyone was my neighbor.

Black church and community members were my watchful extended parents. They applauded me when I did

well and they reported on me when I did wrong. Doing well meant being helpful to others, achieving in school and reading. The only time Daddy would not give me a chore was when I was reading, so I read a lot.

Children were taught by example that nothing was too lowly to do and that the work of our hands and of our heads were both important. Our families and community made us feel useful and important. And while life was often hard and resources scarce, we always knew who we were and that the measure of our worth was inside our heads and hearts, and not outside in personal possessions or ambitions.

I was taught that the world had a lot of problems, that black folk had an extra lot of problems, but that I could struggle and change them; that intellectual and material gifts brought with them the privilege and responsibility of sharing with others less fortunate; and that service is the rent that each of us pays for living — the very purpose of life — and not something you do in your spare time or after you have achieved your personal goals.

I am deeply grateful for these childhood legacies of a living faith reflected in daily service, the discipline of hard work, a capacity to struggle in the face of adversity. Giving up was not part of my childhood lexicon. You got up every morning and did what you had to do, and you got up every time you fell down, and you tried as many times as you had to until you got it done right. My elders

had grit. They valued family life and rituals and tried to be, and expose us to, good role models.

Role models were of two kinds. First were those who had achieved in the outside world, like my namesake, Marian Anderson. The ones I remember most were those who did not have much formal education or money but who taught us by the special grace of their lives, Christ's and Tolstoy's and Gandhi's and Dorothy Day's and King's message, that the Kingdom of God is within. They knew instinctively what Walker Percy wrote, that you can get all A's and still flunk life.

I was fourteen the night Daddy died. He had holes in his shoes, yet two children who had graduated from college, one child in college, another in divinity school, and a vision that he was able to convey to me even dying in an ambulance that I, a young black girl, could be and do anything, that race and gender are shadows, and that character, self-discipline, determination, attitude, and service are the substance of life.

I want to convey that same vision to you today as you graduate into an ethically polluted nation where instant sex without responsibility, instant gratification without effort, instant solutions without sacrifice, getting rather than giving, and hoarding rather than sharing are the too-frequent signals of our mass media, popular culture, and political life.

The standard for success for too many Americans

has become personal greed rather than common good. The standard for striving and achievement has become getting by rather than making an extra effort or helping somebody else. Truth telling and moral example have become devalued commodities. And nowhere is the paralysis of public or private conscience more evident than in the neglect and abandonment of millions of our shrinking pool of children, whose futures more than any other factor will determine our nation's ability to compete and lead in the new era.

Yet every eight seconds of every school day an American child drops out. These are all of our children, not just poor and minority children. Every twenty-six seconds an American child will run away from home. Every thirteen seconds an American child will be abused or neglected. Every sixty-four seconds an American teenager will have a baby. Every seven minutes one of our children is arrested for a drug offense. Every thirty minutes an American child is arrested for drunken driving. Every fifty-three minutes in our rich land an American child dies from the effects of poverty.

It is disgraceful that we permit children to be the poorest Americans. And despite our nearly 300-billion-dollar military defense, we seem not to be able to protect our children from being murdered every three hours. I believe that this great nation can keep its children safe on the streets, in their homes, and in their schools. If we do not do that, what are we about?

I think that our nation is at war at home. As communism is collapsing all around the world, the American dream is collapsing all around America. While tens of thousands of poor young people growing up in inner-city war zones see their futures as a choice between prison and death, many of our middle-class young people are increasingly seeing the future as a choice between a house and a child.

I think we have lost our sense of what is important as a people. Too many young people of all races and classes are growing up without hope and without steady compasses, unable to handle life and navigate a world that is reinventing itself at an unpredictable pace both technologically and politically.

My generation learned that to accomplish anything we had to get off the dime. Your generation must learn to get off the paradigm over and over again and to be flexible, quick, and smart about it.

But I know that despite the dazzling changes that you and all of us are experiencing, there are some enduring values. I feel strongly that it is the responsibility of every adult to make sure that young people hear what we have learned from the lessons of life — what we value most — and that we love you very much and that as you go out into the world you are never alone. I also want to share a few lessons of life taken from a letter that I wrote my own three wonderful sons. Like them, I recognize that you can take or leave them, but you cannot say you

were never told or reminded. Let me give you a few of them.

The first lesson is, there is no free lunch. Do not feel entitled to anything you do not sweat or struggle for. Help our nation understand that it is not entitled to world leadership based on the past or on what we say rather than how well we perform and meet changing world needs.

For those African-American, Latino, Asian-American, and Native American graduates among you today, I want you to remember that you can never take anything for granted in America, even with a college degree. You had better start now, as racial intolerances resurge all over our land. Some of it is as blatant as David Duke or Willie Horton or Rodney King's jury, but some of it is wrapped up in new euphemisms and better etiquette. But as Frederick Douglass warned us earlier, it is the same old snake.

If there are any white graduates among you who feel entitled to leadership by accident of birth, let me remind you that the world you face is already two-thirds nonwhite and poor and that our nation is becoming a mosaic of greater diversity that you are going to have to understand and respect and survive in.

Only two out of every ten new labor-force entrants in the 1990s will be white males born in America. I hope each of you will struggle to achieve and not think for a moment that you have it made. Your degree will get you into the door, but it will not get you to the top of the ca-

reer ladder or keep you there. You have got to work your way up hard and continuously.

Remember not to be lazy. Do your homework. Pay attention to detail. Take care and pride in your work. Take the initiative in creating your own opportunity and do not wait around for other people to discover you or do you a favor. Do not assume a door is closed; push on it. Do not assume if it was closed yesterday that it is closed today. And do not ever stop learning and improving your mind, because if you do, you and America are going to be left behind.

Lesson two is, assign yourself. Daddy used to ask us whether the teacher gave us any homework and if we said no, he said, well, assign yourself some. Do not wait around for somebody else to direct you to do what you are able to figure out and do for yourself. Do not do just as little as you can do to get by.

Do not be a political bystander or grumbler. Vote. Democracy is not a spectator sport. Run for political office. I especially want women to run for political office. We women certainly cannot do a worse job than the men in power now. But when you do run and when you do win, don't begin to think that you or your reelection are the only point. If you see a need, do not ask why doesn't somebody do something, ask why don't I do something. Hard work and persistence and initiative are still the non-magic carpets to success for most of us.

Lesson three: Never work just for money. Money

will not save your soul or build a decent family or help you sleep at night. We are the richest nation on earth with the highest incarceration and one of the highest drug addiction and child poverty rates in the world.

Do not confuse wealth or fame with character. Do not tolerate or condone moral corruption or violence, whether it is found in high or low places, whatever its color or class. It is not okay to push or to use drugs even if every person in America is doing it. It is not okay to cheat or to lie even if every public- and private-sector official you know does. Be honest and demand that those who represent you be honest. Do not confuse morality with legality. Dr. King once noted that everything Hitler did in Nazi Germany was legal. Do not give anyone the proxy for your conscience.

Lesson four: Do not be afraid of taking risks or being criticized. If you do not want to be criticized, do not do anything, do not say anything, and do not be anything. Do not be afraid of failing. It is the way you learn to do things right. It doesn't matter how many times you fall down. All that matters is how many times you get up. Do not wait for everybody to come along to get something done. It is always a few people who get things done and keep things going.

This country desperately needs more wise and courageous shepherds and fewer sheep who do not borrow from integrity to fund expediency.

Lesson five: Take parenting and family life seriously, and insist that those you work for and who represent you do so. Our nation mouths family values which we do not practice or honor in our policies.

Seventy nations provide medical care and financial assistance to all pregnant women. We are not one of them. Seventeen industrialized nations have paid maternity/paternity leave programs. We are not one of them. Our nation alone, among the wealthy, industrialized nations, does not provide for quality early childhood and family support for all our families.

It is time for the mothers and the caring fathers of this nation to tell our political leaders to get with it and stop the political hypocrisy so that all parents can have a real choice about whether to remain at home or to work outside the home without worrying about the safety of their children.

I hope, too, that your generation will raise your sons to be fair to other people's daughters, and to share. I am the mother of three sons, so I have told them that I want them to "share" and not just help with parenting responsibilities.

I hope that you will stress family rituals and be moral examples for your children, because if you cut corners, they will, too. If you lie, they will, too. If you spend all of your money on yourself and tithe no portion of it for your university or civic causes or religious life, they will

not, either. If you tell racial or gender jokes or snicker at them, another generation will pass on the poison that our adult generation still does not have the courage to stop doing.

Lesson six is to please remember and help America remember that the fellowship of human beings is more important than the fellowship of race and class and gender in a democratic society. Be decent and fair and insist that others do so in your presence. Do not tell, do not laugh at or acquiesce in racial, ethnic, religious, or gender jokes or any practice intended to demean rather than enhance another human being. Walk away from them. Make them unacceptable in your presence. Through daily acts of moral consciousness, counter the proliferating voices of racial, ethnic, and religious division that are gaining respectability over our land. And let us face up to rather than ignore our ongoing racial problems, which are America's historical and future Achilles' heel. If we do not heal it, it is going to kill us.

And let us not spend a lot of time uselessly pinning and denying blame rather than healing our divisions. Rabbi Abraham Heschel put it aptly. He said, "We are not all equally guilty, but we are all equally responsible for building a decent and just America."

Lesson seven: Listen for "the sound of the genuine" within yourself. Einstein said, "Small is the number of them that see with their own eyes and feel with their own heart." Try to be one of them.

Howard Thurman, the great black theologian, said to my Spelman colleagues in Atlanta, "There is in every one of us something that waits and listens for the sound of the genuine in ourselves, and it is the only true guide you'll ever have. And if you cannot hear it, you will all of your life spend your days on the ends of strings that somebody else pulls."

You will find as you go out from this place so many noises and competing demands in your lives that many of you may never find out who you are. I hope that you will learn to be quiet enough to hear the sound of the genuine within yourself so that you can then hear it in other people.

Lesson eight: Never think life is not worth living or that you cannot make a difference. Never give up. I do not care how hard it gets; and it will get very hard sometimes. An old proverb reminds us that when you get to your wit's end, remember that is where God lives.

Harriet Beecher Stowe said that when you get into a tight place and everything goes against you, till it seems as though you cannot hang on for another minute, never give up then, for that is just the place and the time the tide will turn.

I do not care how bad the job market is. I do not care how hard the challenges seem to be. Hang in with life. And do not think you have to win or win immediately or even at all to make a difference. Sometimes it is important

to lose the things that matter. And do not think you have to make a big difference to make America different.

My role model was an illiterate slave woman, Sojourner Truth, who could not read or write, but she could not stand second-class treatment of women and she hated slavery. My favorite Sojourner story came one day when she was making a speech against slavery and she got heckled by a man who stood up in the audience and said, "Old slave woman, I don't care any more about your antislavery talk than for an old fleabite." And she snapped back and said, "That's all right. The Lord willing, I'm going to keep you scratching."

So often we think we have got to make a big difference and be a big dog. Let us just try to be little fleas biting. Enough fleas biting strategically can make very big dogs very uncomfortable. I am convinced that together fleas for justice and fleas in schools and religious congregations and fleas in homes as parents committed to a decent American society are going to transform our nation in the 1990s and make it un-American for any child to be poor or without health care in our rich land.

Finally, let me just hope that you will understand that you cannot save your own children without trying to help save other people's children. They have got to walk the same streets. We have got to pass on to them a country that was better than the one that we inherited. This nation

has got to stop making a distinction between our children and other people's children.

I want to end with a prayer by a schoolteacher who said, "Let's pray and accept responsibility for those children who like to be tickled and eat Popsicles before supper and can never find their shoes; but let's also commit to praying and advocating for those children who can't bound down the street in a new pair of sneakers, who never get dessert, who don't have any rooms to clean up, whose pictures aren't on anybody's dressers, and whose monsters are real."

Let us commit as you go out into the world, praying and accepting responsibility for children who spend all of their allowance before Tuesday, who throw tantrums in the grocery store and pick at their food, who squirm in church or temple and scream in the phone. But it is also important that you go out and pray and accept responsibility for children whose nightmares come in the daytime, who will eat anything but who have never seen a dentist, are not spoiled by anybody, go to bed hungry, and cry themselves to sleep.

Let us commit to praying and accepting responsibility for children who want to be carried, but also for those children who need to be carried, for those we never give up on and for those that do not get a second chance. Let us pray and fight and vote for those children whom we

smother, but also for those children who will grab the hand of anybody kind enough to offer it.

What do you think would happen if every American, if every one of you, reached out and grabbed the hand of a child and committed to seeing that no child is left behind? I hope that you will think about doing that, because everything that we hold dear as a people with faith depends on each of us committing to leaving no American child behind.

ROBERT FULGHUM

Known to the general public for his best-seller, *All I Really Need to Know I Learned in Kindergarten*, Robert Fulghum is not only an author but a musician, sculptor, painter, and philosopher. Prior to his writing career, he studied theology extensively and served as a Unitarian minister for twenty-two years. While riding the rodeo circuit in his youth, he also worked as a ranch hand and a singing cowboy. Fulghum was born in 1937, was raised in Waco, Texas, and now lives in Seattle on a houseboat. In addition to his books, he began a syndicated newspaper column in November 1994, and is involved in raising money for charities.

ROBERT FULGHUM

Smith College
Northampton, Massachusetts
May 19, 1991

This is a letter from a college student to her mother and father:

Dear Mom and Dad,

I'm sorry I haven't written in a long time, but something I smoked seemed to have affected my eyesight for a while. The problem is better now. When I was in the emergency room I met a really fine man. He gave me some crystals to meditate on, and, well, to make a long story short, you'll soon have your wish of becoming grandparents. Don't worry. He's mature; he's twenty years older than I am and he has a steady job at the hospital. Who knows, we might even get married. I knew that you would want to be the first to know.

P.S. I really didn't do any drugs, and I wasn't in the hospital, and I'm not pregnant. I don't even have a boyfriend. But I did

flunk chemistry. I just wanted you to view
this problem in proper perspective.

That is an old story that is brought up to date. It is a
metaphor for this occasion — which is an old story brought
up to date, a rite of passage, a ritual that you have not experienced before but which human beings have been
doing for a long, long time.

I suspect that you know just about everything that
you can hold for the moment in the way of information
and advice, and you have some time to process that now.
So I will not, unlike some speakers, give you advice and
tell you about the future. What I would like to give you as
a gift is two stories. Stories that you might take with you
as a peg to hang on the wall of your life, so that long
days after this, when you assimilate the experiences that
you had at this institution, you might have this peg to hang
it on.

The first story comes from a friend of mine who is
a kindergarten teacher — one of the best. She was asked at
a teacher's convention if she would have her class act out
some myth, fairy tale, or other good story. So being the
good teacher that she was, instead of deciding herself, she
went to the students, her kindergarten class, and said, "The
teachers would like us to act something out. What would
you like to do?" And after a lot of discussion, not to anybody's real surprise, they picked something very old. A

story that the whole human race knows. They picked that classic old chestnut of "Cinderella."

It is interesting to note in passing that no matter when the survey is taken, that remains the most popular fairy tale for all ages. In the United States of America at least.

It was a good choice on the part of the children because there are lots of roles in "Cinderella." And lots of flexibility. So there was this sorting out that had to be done: Who wanted to be Cinderella — all the girls wanted to be the princess — and who wanted to be the coachman, and on and on. As the children received a role and sorted this out among themselves, they were labeled as useful in what their role was and sent over to the side of the room. Until there was only one child left: a small kid, tubby, not particularly involved with the other kids in the class — in fact, sometimes teased — sort of a different kid. The teacher could not say why, but he was not quite like the rest. So she said to him — his name was Norman — "Norman, what are you going to be?" "Well," said Norman, "I think I will be the pig." The teacher said, "Norman, there is no pig in the story of 'Cinderella.'" And Norman said, "Well, there is now."

So they left it to Norman as to what was the pig's part. I mean, no one quite knew how to fit a pig into the story of "Cinderella." It turns out that Norman knew exactly what his part was. It was one of the great walk-on parts of all time.

His notion was to go with Cinderella wherever she went and do whatever she did. So Norman was always there — sort of a porcine Greek chorus to the events. Norman had nothing to say, but Norman's face reflected the action of the drama. When things were serious, he was serious. When things looked worrisome, he looked worried. When things were in doubt, he looked anxious. He began to fill the stage with his presence of response by simply sitting there. And at the end of the performance when the princess was carried off to live happily ever after, Norman stood on his hind legs and barked.

In rehearsal this had been troublesome because the teacher said, "Look, Norman, even if there is a pig in the story, pigs do not bark." And Norman said, "Well, this one does."

You can imagine what happened the night of the performance. There was a standing ovation at the end for the pig. Norman, the barking pig, who was, as it turns out, the Cinderella in the story after all.

Word gets around, and people called up the teacher and said, "We hear you have this dynamite Cinderella thing. What is so special about it?" She said, "Well, there is a pig in it — actually, a barking pig." And the person on the other end of the telephone would say, "But there is no barking pig in 'Cinderella.'" And the teacher would say with great conviction, "Well, there is now."

I went out to visit Sophia Smith's grave this morn-

ing, to see her house, and I realized that she was a barking pig. She said that there should be a college for women, and people said there is no such thing as a college for women. Her response was, "Well, there is now."

I have always thought that the "Cinderella" story was poison — especially the one that is loose in our culture — because it describes a young woman whose position in life is to wait — to wait for the prince, to wait for the fairy godmother. The sweatshirt that Cinderella wore says, "Maybe something will happen." Norman, the barking pig, is the kind of "Cinderella" story I like because Norman got up and demanded that there be room for him and his image of himself in this world. And the real fairy godmother was the teacher who recognized the truth that Norman was reaching for and had affirmed his place in the scheme of things. That is a fairy story you can count on.

Hold that thought for a minute — of Norman the barking pig — and let me tell you another story to lay alongside it to take with you.

This past spring I was in a town not much bigger than this one, maybe an hour's train ride south and west of Paris. It is a town I am sure some of you have visited, and I hope in the future more of you will go. This is where the great Gothic cathedral of Chartres is built. It is probably the most magnificent statement in stone and stained glass that exists on the face of this earth.

The story about Chartres again is an old story that

needs to be brought up to date. The story goes that some time during its building, in the early days, a visitor from Rome stopped by to see this amazing thing that was happening in this small town. He got there at the end of the day, and he went into the unfinished structure, and he began to bump into workmen as they were leaving. One of them was brushing some stuff off his front, and the visitor asked him, "What do you do?" And the man said, "Oh, I make glass windows." The visitor went a little further and he bumped into someone else who was brushing sawdust off himself. He asked, "What do you do?" The man said, "I am a woodworker. I am making some beams over here." A little further back, someone else was brushing dust off of himself as he headed home for the evening. Again, the question was, "What do you do?" The answer was, "I am cutting some stone."

Finally the visitor got as far back in this great structure as he could go, and there was an older woman with some young people. They were cleaning up and sweeping and putting tools away. The visitor asked this woman who was doing this work, "What do you do?" She looked at these young people, and she looked at the structure rising above her, and then she said, "Me? I am building a cathedral for the glory of God."

She had a perspective on her place in the scheme of things. And though it was not grand by title — not architect, not mason, not stained glass window maker — she

had a perception of her place in the scheme of things. "Me? I am building a cathedral for the glory of God." She, too, was a barking pig, like Norman — one of his distant cousins.

I give you these two stories to cast a perspective on what you do when you go from this place. This institution at its very finest is in the business of helping barking pigs find their place. This institution in its every part — staff, faculty, parents, students, and visitors — is not just a school but part of that human endeavor of building, if not a cathedral for the glory of God, at least an invisible cathedral for the best in the human spirit.

The thing that strikes me about the cathedral at Chartres is that town was no bigger than this one — 35,000 people, give or take. And they built this incredible thing. The other amazing thing about the building of Chartres is that they started something that they knew they would never see finished. But if they did not start it, it would not ever be finished, and so they began.

Sophia Smith also started something that she would never see finished. It would be a wonderful thing if she could see this campus and see you here, but she just had to begin it. And now the next stage of the process is carrying it on. One hundred years from now, when you lie where she lies, may it be that others like you are still here finishing the cathedral that is Smith College and the larger cathedral that is the spirit of humanity of self. For all your

affirmation of being women, you are above all in the business of becoming and making whole human beings.

If I had the social courage, I would have simply brought a mirror here this afternoon and held it up and said, "look." But I realize the mirror is here. The mirror is these people back here — your faculty. When you look at them you see an awful lot of yourself. And you are a mirror for them, for when they look at you they see the best of themselves. And there are mirrors over here called parents who look at you and see themselves, and you are reflected in them and in friends and family. This place is full of mirrors, reflecting back the amazing world of barking pigs and cathedral builders that we all are.

I said I would not give you advice, and I would simply pass on that reflection to you. I leave the rest of the thinking that comes from those two stories up to you.

I would like to make a personal request. For my own strange reasons, I did not go on to have an academic degree laid on me. But I am a practical man, and so I would like to request from this class and the administration of this college that you give me the gift of this chair, this very chair, so that long days from now I can sit in it, and it will bring to mind this lovely day, this amazing institution, this sweet life, and the remarkable and unforgettable company of all of you.

94

CATHY GUISEWITE

Cathy Guisewite is the creator of the internationally syndicated cartoon strip "Cathy," which she began in 1976. The cartoon has earned countless awards for its unique view of life and women's issues. In addition to producing her cartoon strip, she illustrates books and runs her own licensing agency for products bearing her comic strip's character. In 1993, she was awarded "Outstanding Cartoonist of the Year" by the National Cartoonists Society. Guisewite's success has brought her national media attention, dozens of television appearances, and product endorsements. In 1987, her animated program, *Cathy*, won an Emmy award. Born in Dayton, Ohio, in 1950, she now lives and works in the Los Angeles area.

CATHY GUISEWITE

University of Michigan
Ann Arbor, Michigan
April 30, 1994

The fact that the University of Michigan would have a commencement speaker who has publicly admitted to hiding in the ladies' room with a box of doughnuts as a way of coping with business pressure means a lot to me. The committee was also willing to overlook the fact that I balance my checkbook by switching banks and starting all over every six months . . . that I sometimes call in sick because I can't get my hair straight . . . and that I end each day in my brilliant career with a tiny, secret prayer that my desk will burn down in the night.

This is a school that understands that success is not something we achieve once and get to keep, but something we have to each re-earn in our own way every day.

This is a school that understands that every hope, every dream, and every single speck of your fabulous education still has to be filtered through you. The human element . . . that your ability to cope daily with the little stuff is going to have as much to do with how your future works as the four years you just spent getting your degree.

The world expects so much of you. You will be expected to be a dynamic businessperson; financial wizard;

nurturing homemaker; enlightened, involved parent; environmental activist; physical fitness expert; a sexy and alluring yet responsible partner; champion of human rights; independent thinker; community activist; and if you're a woman, a size 5, all at once.

Today, when the message is that anyone can do anything, it is going to be very hard not to feel that everyone else is doing something, and that you personally are standing still in the same old ruts.

It is already hard not to get the impression that everyone else is coping better, isn't it? Everyone seems more efficient, more organized, more confident.

Everyone else not only knew how to get to North Campus but knew there was one. Everyone else knew it was a mistake to sign up for the 8:00 A.M. art history lecture, where the first thing they do is turn out all the lights and start talking about dream visions.

Everyone has a better direction, a better love life, a better day planner, and a better therapist . . . not to mention a clue what they are going to do tomorrow. It is hard not to be depressed by the very examples that are supposed to inspire you.

And just in case normal human insecurity does not nail you when you get out in the world, you will be bombarded by images which, even when you know better than to believe them, will do their little number on your brains.

Look at how women are bombarded in 1994. Look

at the commercials. Look at how they picture men and women. The men are still doing one thing in the commercials. The women are doing six things at once.

The man in the commercial is mowing the lawn. One job. The woman is giving herself a beauty treatment for her hands while she does the dishes. The man is grilling a steak. One job. The woman is simultaneously cleaning the oven, disinfecting the floor, popping a five-course meal in the microwave, and faxing the office while explaining the magic of feminine hygiene products to her daughter.

If you think that does not translate into real-life expectations, head for Detroit during rush hour some morning and look around you on the freeway. The men are driving to work. One job. The women are driving to work, steering the car with their knees, applying eyeliner with one hand, rehemming their power suits with the other hand, singing songs to the children they are dropping off at day care, while listening to French language tapes and doing isometric butt exercises.

We like to believe that women are equals in the workplace, but to even look acceptable for her first interview, a woman will spend more on her haircut, more on her makeup, more on her underwear, more on her shoes, and more on her outfit, which will take a hundred times more time to get together, since the pieces are in twelve different departments and women's stores do not do alterations, and five minutes after the Visa bill arrives the

woman will have to start all over again because it all just went out of style.

It is a microcosm of the extra expectations that come with being a woman, and the extra sense of isolation that many women will feel when they try to do everything and cannot.

Compounding the loneliness for many women has been the fact that if we expressed any vulnerability in the process of trying to live up to fifty images at once, we were shaming our gender by being stereotypically weak.

Men are bombarded with their own set of impossible images. They have been honed and handed down by a zillion generations of protectors and providers and have smacked head-on into a world which is simultaneously screaming for and rejecting the kinder, gentler kind of guy.

A lot of my work as a cartoonist revolves around coping with the pressures that result from the images, trying to close the gap between who we are supposed to be, versus who we want to be, versus who we actually were at 7:30 this morning.

I have searched for answers. I have prayed for inspiration. I have begged for miracles. I have scoured the mall. I humbly offer the four clues I have so far.

1. *Give up the quest for perfection and shoot for five good minutes in a row.* When I came to the University of Michigan as a freshman, I was five pounds overweight and desperate to lose the weight immediately so I would be liked

by each of my 34,000 classmates. My first crash diet resulted in a gain of four more pounds, and then I was really desperate. I quit eating completely for three days.

I slipped into a Diet Coke-induced delusionary stupor during my first all-nighter and gained another seven pounds when I accidentally ordered and ate pizza for the entire Mosher-Jordon Dorm.

I vowed to not only lose the weight instantly but to look my demons directly in the eye, so I got a job at Drakes, where I gained another twenty-nine pounds, for a grand total of forty-five pounds by the end of my senior year, which I figure means my college education cost my parents a thousand dollars a pound.

In retrospect, it all could have gone so differently if I had just refrained from eating for five minutes in a row. The only thing I have ever succeeded at instantly was failing.

Every one of you knows someone who did better than you at something in college because they approached it with a slow, steady, dignified attack, rather than going for the screaming, end-of-semester, bluebook miracle.

A lot of what you just experienced at the University of Michigan is unfortunately exactly how it works on the outside. Just like in college, you will be able to luck out now and then and get an A without trying, but if you bank on that as your system, you will flunk life in general. Just like in college, you will be tempted to take on too much at once and will have diminished results in all the categories.

Just like in college, you will eventually have to do your laundry and call your parents to beg for money. And mostly, just like in college, you will be graded not for how dramatic your plans are but for what you actually sit down and do, slowly, deliberately, for five minutes in a row. If you can succeed for five minutes in a row, you can do anything.

2. *Remember what you love.* I know that a lot of your parents are here, and that this day means as much to them as it does to you. Graduation is the sort of rich, precious, intensely emotional day that has always brought out the very worst in my family. In the eight hours I spent with them on Graduation Day, we managed to have a miniature recap of every psychodrama we had had since I arrived here as a freshman.

It took us two and one-half hours to buy a cup of coffee in the cafeteria line in the Union the morning of my graduation. My father wanted to take a picture of Mom and me in line. My mother said no, that my dad should be in the picture, and that she would take it. My father said my mother always cuts off everyone's head, and that he should take all the pictures.

Neither one of them could get the flash to work, so I said I would take the picture. At this point there were twenty people backed up in line behind us, and all twenty were pleading to take our picture as a group and be done with it.

Mom did not want to inconvenience anyone, so she

said she would take everyone else's picture and started simultaneously snapping shots and looking for a pencil so she could write down their names and addresses to send them copies.

Dad felt guilty that Mom was decapitating an entire group of strangers with her photography and offered to buy doughnuts for everyone in line. Mom worried that there were now thirty-five people getting crumbs on the floor and went into the kitchen to get a broom so she could help sweep.

I stood in the middle and just started shrieking, "This is who I am! This is the gene pool! This is why I never get anything done!"

By the end of Graduation Day, it was as though we had assembled our own little psychological parent-child yearbook. When I flip through the pages of that yearbook now, I see the tangle of love and impatience and dependence and defiance that makes up the most important relationship of my life. When I look at my family, I know who I am.

But it is more than just family. The experience of going to the University of Michigan bonds people in a bizarre way that I can only describe by saying that even though I did not graduate with a big circle of friends in my class, almost all the people who have become my best friends since college went to school here and graduated at different times.

I did not even know them when I was here, and

every single one of them has helped keep me more connected to what I believe in than anyone else I have met. Every single one of them came here today to be at your graduation with me. One of my friends who not only came to your graduation but brought his whole family is Larry Kasdan, who wrote *The Big Chill* and told the whole world about the depth of friendship and connection that happens on this campus.

Every year you are out of school you will have more names in your phone book and fewer actual friends. A lot of the ones that really count will be people who mapped out their dreams on the diag just like you. When I look at my friends from the University of Michigan, I believe in who I am.

But it is not just friends and family. You might not even realize it today, but each one of you has had one pivotal experience here that will eventually define what you do with the rest of your life. I am talking about the kind of experience that felt so right, was so exhilarating, tapped into your essence in such a way that you will look back on it and say, "That was the moment my calling was revealed to me."

My pivotal experience at the University of Michigan was the book *Ulysses.* The two-million-page, twenty-pound masterpiece *Ulysses,* which I took one entire, semester-long class on. I never read the book. I never made it through the "Cliff Notes." I went into Angel Hall for my written essay final on *Ulysses* knowing only that it

had something to do with a guy in Ireland. I left Angel Hall an hour and fifteen minutes later with an A in the class and the knowledge that I had a gift for creative writing.

The exhilaration of creating ten poignant, insightful pages out of nothing but complete hysteria is what convinced me I should write for a living; and that reconvinces me every time I remember it. When I look at my *Ulysses* bluebook twenty-two years later, I trust who I am.

Look at what you love on graduation day. Take the classes, the friends, and the family that have inspired the most in you. Save them in your permanent memory and make a backup disk. When you remember what you love, you will remember who you are. If you remember who you are, you can do anything.

3. *If you want something to change, do something different.* When I look back and think about the things I could have done and should have done and wish I had said and wanted to try and thought of changing, time and time again I see the only brick walls that were ever really in my way were the ones I lovingly built myself, brick by brick, and then proceeded to smash my head against. I just could not get out of my own way.

Stuck with myself, I have had no choice but to do some deep, introspective thinking, and like so many bright, intelligent Americans, to really search my own soul until I found a way to blame someone else.

I blame the products I buy for funding the TV

channels I subscribe to for desensitizing me to violence. I blame the company I paid a fortune to for my car for mucking up my air. I blame the fashion industry I spend thousands on for degrading women, leaving me with the sickening feeling that I am financing my own destruction, which, of course, I blame on the politicians whose salaries I pay, which I lump into a pool with all the other miscellaneous unpleasantries of life and blame on my parents.

If people responded honestly to everything that was simultaneously going wrong in their own lives and in the world on any given day, we would all just run around screaming all the time.

On a personal level, it is hard to make changes because of the fear that if we change, something might be different. In the world at large, it is hard to make changes because of the fear that no matter what we do, nothing will be different. And in both cases, we are hit with the bonus fear that even if things are different, they will be worse.

I graduated with a class committed to open love, open thinking, open doors, open everything. Twenty-two years later a whole generation of flower children are spending four thousand dollars each on burglar alarms for our cars and homes so that no one will take our things.

My graduating class rejected the depersonalized greed of corporate structure. We believed in people. Our goal was to understand people, to relate to people, nothing would ever come before the people. Twenty-two years later

the people of my class are getting cash out of a machine, dinner out of a clown's mouth, and it is not even possible to get a human being on the phone at the phone company. In Los Angeles, my only chance of having a meaningful encounter with a person is if I smash into one with my car.

My graduating class demanded information. We wanted to know why our revolution was backfiring. We got 150 cable channels. One third are eyewitness crime shows. One third are entertainment crime shows. One third are news commentary shows, showing in graphic detail how all the crime shows are warping our minds and creating the next generation of little villains.

I have fantasized that I could really change and have an impact if I could just move to a different city, take on a new identity and start fresh, where everyone, including me, did not already know what sort of person I was. Every single person in the audience who is not graduating today is jealous of the fact that most of you who are graduating get to do just that.

We all appreciate that it will not be that easy. You have grown up in a strange time where people seem more bonded by the bad stuff than the good, where in a lot of communities the main common link between neighbors is that everyone knows someone who has AIDS, everyone knows someone who has been mugged, everyone knows someone in rehab, and everyone has been touched by a life that ended way too soon.

If you want something to change, you personally have to do something different. You have to take a stand when it is not convenient. Say something in a relationship when it hurts to do it. Work harder than you are used to working. Try something nobody else has tried. Defy your own group. Rebel against yourself. Knock down your walls and get out of your own way. If you are brave enough to do something different, you can do anything.

4. *Let yourself regraduate every four years.* In one of my mother's really annoying moments of being right about something, Mom told me that life deserves an overhaul every four years. She said four years is exactly enough time in any situation to know what is working, what is not, what is worth saving, and what or who you ought to dump. As with most of her advice, I staged my own personal rebellion and hung onto everything I ever owned, clung to relationships way past when it was appropriate, and not only settled into ruts but dug them so deep they became like little subterranean villages stuffed with cable TV and bad habits.

In another really annoying moment of being right about something, my mother quit mentioning the four-year-overhaul thing completely a few years ago, which forced me to rebel again and bring it up myself and, even though I was twenty years overdue, to stage my own overhaul.

When I took a really good hard look at things, I saw that I was great at my career, horrible at personal relation-

ships, and that I had fifteen minutes left in which to meet someone, fall in love, get married, get pregnant, and have a child, if I ever wanted to be a parent. I used the full fifteen minutes I had left on my biological clock to call my mother and scream at her for not being pushy enough. I then started the process that eventually resulted in my adopting a beautiful baby girl named Ivy.

Adopting Ivy was without question the hardest and loneliest thing I have ever done. I had to change every single fantasy about how I thought I would have a child, who I thought I would have a child with, how I thought a family should work, not to mention change every single minute of how I was used to living.

Twenty years after getting down on my hands and knees and begging my University of Michigan Spanish professor to pass me out of the language requirement that I would never use, I have had to sign up for a Spanish Berlitz course so I could keep up with what my two-year-old is learning on *Sesame Street*. Like many psychotic, exhausted mothers, I can only say that if I had it to do all over again I only wish I would have done it a little bit sooner.

Let yourself regraduate every four years. Celebrate what you have done. Admit what you are not doing. Think about what is important to you and make some changes. If you give yourself a chance to move on, you can do anything.

For all the women and men of the class of 1994,

the only thing greater than the frustration of attempting to do it all will be the seduction of wanting to try.

Both personally and professionally, I believe very strongly in visualizing goals way beyond what seems humanly possible. I got this from my parents, who are great dreamers themselves and always insisted my sisters and I could do anything, way past the point of all logic.

When my mother first suggested I submit some scribbles to a comic-strip syndicate, I pointed out that I knew nothing about comic-strip syndicates or comic strips. Mom said, so what? You will learn.

When I submitted my scribbles to a comic-strip syndicate and I pointed out to Mom that I did not know how to draw, she said, so what? You will learn.

When the syndicate sent me a contract to do a comic strip for them, I asked Mom how she thought I could possibly think of something worth printing 365 days a year for the next forty years. Mom took me by the hand, sat me down at a table, and together we ate a Sara Lee cheesecake.

All parents believe their children can do the impossible. They thought it the minute we were born, and no matter how hard we have tried to prove them wrong, they all think it about us now. And the really annoying thing is, they are probably all right again.

You are no different from the graduate sitting next

to you who might solve the world's energy problems. You are no different from the one behind you who might bring about the most important changes yet in human rights. You are no different from the one in front of you who might inspire all of our children with his or her brilliant teaching.

Each of us wages a private battle each day between the grand fantasies we have for ourselves and what actually happens. Between the graceful, meaningful way others seem to use their time, versus the chaos of our own.

We all have to learn to not give up if we are not perfect tomorrow and to somehow stay optimistic that we will be perfect the day after tomorrow.

As graduates, you have to set standards for how you work, how you treat others, how you let yourself be treated. You have to simultaneously celebrate yourself and rebel against yourself. You have to defy your group, knock down your walls, and get out of your own way. You have to separate yourself from the 10,000 things that are expected of you and concentrate on something one day at a time. I suggest these four clues to start:

1. *Give up the quest for perfection and shoot for five good minutes in a row.*

2. *Remember what you love.*

3. *If you want something to change, do something different.*

4. *Let yourself regraduate every four years.*

And when you are demoralized, with no hope in your heart and a pint of Häagen-Dazs in your stomach, crawl over to the box of junk you never quite got organized, pull out your diploma, and remember the best clue of all:

If you made it through this place, you can do anything.

DANIEL K. INOUYE

Senator Daniel K. Inouye has served Hawaii in various political offices since 1959, when he was elected to the United States House of Representatives as Hawaii's first congressman. He won reelection in 1960 and was later elected to the United States Senate, in 1962. Senator Inouye played a major role in the defense policies of the United States through his membership in the Defense Subcommittee of the Senate. During his tenure in the Senate, he fought for improved education for all children, better health care for Hawaiians, diversified agriculture in the islands, and measures that helped protect and preserve Hawaii's natural resources. He was born in 1924 in Honolulu, Hawaii.

DANIEL K. INOUYE

The University of Hawaii
Honolulu, Hawaii
December 20, 1992

There are few events on my calendar which so vividly symbolize the hopes and dreams of young America as does the awarding of the baccalaureate — few events which speak so eloquently to the promise which our great nation offers to each of its citizens.

In your transition from student and scholar to graduate, our nation is once again blessed with renewed creativity and the power of youthful idealism. For just as surely as each one of you represents the pinnacle of hope and achievement for your families, so, too, do you represent yet one more jewel in the crown of our great democracy.

This is your moment, your hour, to be recognized for all that you have accomplished during your years of study. It is the first of what I hope will be many golden days in the sun for each one of you. I salute your achievements, take pride in the honor which you bring to all Hawaii, and bid you the best of luck as you move off to new horizons.

Before you go, however, I would like to leave you with a few thoughts about the changing face of the world in which you are now entering — a world of challenge, a

world of opportunity, and yes, a world of increasing uncertainty. The events now unfolding in Asia, Africa, and
Europe suggest that we are embarking upon a period of
tumultuous change — a time of political reorientation as
dramatic and as profound as any which our fathers and
grandfathers witnessed this century.

I wish I could reassure you that the unrest which
now encircles the globe will be short-lived and that peace
and prosperity will be the inevitable consequence of humanity's eternal struggle for justice and equality. This is
certainly my prayer, but unfortunately is beyond the capacity of any of us to predict.

As one who has seen the ravages of war and poverty
numerous times over the course of my life, I would be de-
ceiving you if my optimism for the future were not tem-
pered by what I know to be reality. History provides no
guarantees on the shape of things to come. The possibilities
for good and for evil remain essentially today, as they have
always been, as numerous as the stars.

Yet, if there is anything in this world of which I am
absolutely certain, it is that within each of us lies the
power to transform the world for the better. Let there be
no doubt as to the ability of well-meaning individuals to
change life's odds and to influence his or her own destiny
along a positive course.

If there is any message that I hope you will carry
with you into the future, it is this: You can make a differ-

ence in your lives and in the lives of others if you simply care enough to try and care enough to persevere.

This is the spirit that built our nation and made possible the freedoms we now cherish.

I believe most passionately that in each one of you lies a Jefferson, a Lincoln, an Eleanor Roosevelt, a Mother Teresa, and a Martin Luther King, Jr. None of these great men and women accepted the failures and inequities of the world in which they were born, and neither should you! They believed in the perfectibility of the world in which they lived and would not be turned away from what they knew was good, what was right, and what was just.

This brings me to the state of the world today. It was not so long ago that commencement speakers would have begun an address on the politics of our time by first describing the nuclear face-off between the United States and the Soviet Union. For nearly forty years, the world was viewed through the prism of the Cold War, a war which pitted East against West, good against evil, and communist totalitarianism against democracy. During this period, the fear of nuclear holocaust shaped our national consciousness. The race for new and exotic weapons to meet the rising Soviet threat became all-consuming, defining the course of much of our science and technology development. Perhaps you recall those days — it was just a mere twelve months ago — exactly twelve months since the collapse of the Soviet Union!

Ironically, in the light of current events, these now seem like simpler, less complicated times. National security policy meant deterrence. Nuclear policy meant flexible response. And foreign policy meant containment. What could be more certain than that there would always be a Soviet menace? What could be more inconceivable than the thought of thermonuclear war?

Whether the issue was poverty in the Third World, leftist insurgency, resource depletion, or weapons proliferation, American policy makers could be reasonably sure that all roads led to Moscow. How convenient it was to have a single address for so many of the world's problems.

This is not so today. While the demise of Soviet communism has led to a frenzied rush of democratic nation building, the prospects for the future remain anything but certain. In places as remote as Bosnia, the Georgian Republic, Tajikistan, and Nagorno-Karabakh, liberation from Moscow has brought about none of the stability or prosperity which the citizens of these areas had dreamed of for decades. Instead of peace, civil war, territorial disputes, hyperinflation, and ethnic strife have become the cruel legacy of self-determination.

What has been left in the wake of the once monolithic Soviet empire is a collection of economically and politically depressed ministates, each struggling to survive as democratic nations with little capacity to succeed and

no experience upon which to undertake such a bold experiment.

Once a military giant, the former Soviet Union is today reduced to little more than a weapons supermarket, selling off its once-prized tanks, artillery, and aircraft to any country willing to pay the price. Just recently, Iran purchased three submarines from Moscow, and there are reports that the government of Kazakhstan has sold nuclear warheads, and possibly launchers, to Iran as well.

The reason for this fire sale of the century is simple. Faced with mounting debts, collapsing economies, unemployment, political instability, and the prospect of large-scale starvation, the new republics of Asia have come to rely on the sale of weaponry as virtually the only source of hard currency.

It is a sad fact that, just when humanity appeared to be moving away from armed confrontation, this new influx of weapons into the world's trouble spots has brought about a renewed fear of war, insurgency, and repression. Even the scientists of the former Soviet Union are rushing to sell their services abroad — services which include the manufacture of weapons of mass destruction.

Who could have imagined, just five years ago, that the ethnic, nationalist, and religious strife in places like Abkhazia, South Ossetia, and Bosnia would dominate our headlines and lead to fears of a bloody pandemic, in much

the same way that war suddenly and irrationally engulfed the world in August 1914.

Until a new world order emerges that truly represents a break with the past, we will have to gird ourselves for increasing global instability. The questions are many; the answers, at this time, are few. What will be the future of relations between India and Pakistan, North and South Korea, Iran and Iraq? What new and unpredictable direction can we expect from a changing China, an untamed Libya, or a nuclear Argentina or Brazil?

Our nation is obliged to remain strong and resolute in the face of the changes now taking place. In our rush to demobilize our armed forces and melt down the weapons of war, we must stop to consider just what might be required should the winds of misfortune turn in our direction. Is it prudent, I ask you, to close down the community fire station and sell off its equipment simply because an area has been temporarily spared the ravages of an inferno? Of course not. I know you know better. I trust that the American people know better as well.

This, of course, does not mean that we should not adapt ourselves to the changes taking place both at home and abroad. Clearly, the economic policies of the Cold War are incompatible with the new realities our nation faces. Fiscal austerity will mean a change in the way we deploy our military forces. It will mean a continuing drawdown in the numbers of men and women under arms. Bases shall

close and the size of our nuclear arsenal will decrease. This is how it should be.

In its place, however, we are creating a lighter, more mobile force able to respond to conflict and instability in new and creative ways. The skill and professionalism exhibited by our forces during Operation Desert Storm builds on the experience of the past and is characteristic of the changes now taking place in our armed forces.

Even as we speak, the American military is engaged in vital humanitarian relief work in Somalia, Iraq, Kurdistan, and Bosnia-Herzegovina — essential tasks for which our people are most ably suited. This work, I believe, is just as important to our national security as was manning the watchtowers along the inter-German frontier for nearly forty years, perhaps even more so.

If you had ever been to those stricken areas of the world where our relief teams have been, you would know that they have left behind an enduring legacy of American friendship and caring. It is an impression that, in places like Armenia, the Philippines, and Bangladesh, has entered the folklore and deepest memory of the people we have assisted.

And what of our foreign policy in the years ahead? Here, too, our national perspective is shifting. The Asian-Pacific region, not the Atlantic, has become the principal focus of our international economic life.

Nowhere is this better seen than in the issues surrounding trade with Japan, the transition of Hong Kong to

China in 1997, or the impact of the North American Free Trade Area (NAFTA). In each instance, it is the Pacific region that claims the spotlight in Washington and is the focus of growing concern for policy makers.

There could not have been a more propitious time for you, the graduates of the University of Hawaii, to be studying here in the Aloha State. You live on the frontier of a new age of opportunity and discovery and have imbibed all that this unique perspective has to offer. No group of students in our nation today will have been prepared better for the challenges which lie ahead in this region of the world.

The diversity of numbers and the focus of your curriculum have given you an advantage in the new world of Asian-Pacific culture, commerce, and cooperation that few can match.

In your lifetime, this region, which borders five of the world's seven continents, has become the great meeting place of civilization, the source of critical raw materials and the engine of our global economy. Understanding the needs and addressing the concerns of the people of the Pacific rim is becoming not just an important but an essential requirement for our survival and prosperity as a nation. For though the challenge is enormous, you have been molded by a university of exceptional character and caliber. Its perspective has been influenced, in no small measure, by the scholarship embedded in the East-West Center, an

institution noted for its academic stature and ability, both on the mainland and abroad. For over a quarter of a century, the center has brought our nation closer to understanding the unique and often perplexing cultures and customs of the Pacific region. All Americans owe it a debt of gratitude.

In conclusion, let me say that the greatest of your accomplishments are still before you. Go forth and seek them, give flight to your dreams, take hold the reins of destiny, and live life to the fullest. Aloha.

BILLY JOEL

Born in New York City in 1949, Billy Joel is one of the best-selling solo recording artists of the twentieth century. As a child, he loved and was trained in classical music, but his renditions of Beethoven were soon transformed, building the foundation for his career. After seeing the Beatles perform on *The Ed Sullivan Show*, his dream to become a professional musician grew. He started performing professionally in junior high and worked at numerous odd jobs to make ends meet. He recorded his first album in 1972, and an incredibly successful career followed, with numerous worldwide concert tours and Grammy awards. Joel now spends a great deal of time on charity concerts and often collaborates with other artists in concerts and recordings.

BILLY JOEL

Fairfield University
Fairfield, Connecticut
May 19, 1991

When I was first asked to speak to the graduating class of
Fairfield University, my initial reaction was not too dissimilar
to a certain philosophy professor who is a member of the
faculty here. I had to ask myself, What makes me qualified
to do this? What relevance do I have to the future lives of
these young people? After all, I did not even go to college,
and I did write a song called "Only the Good Die Young."
So, why me?

After meeting with a group of Fairfield students, I
realized what I might be able to share with you from my
perspective. I have lived what many would consider to be
an unorthodox life, but it has always been an interesting one.

It is true that I did not graduate from high school;
but like you, I did spend years majoring in my own area of
study. I am a graduate of the University of Rock and Roll,
Class of 1970. My diploma was a check — a week's worth
of wages earned from playing long nights in smoky, crowded
clubs in the New York area. Through the years, I have been
given platinum albums, Grammys, keys to cities, and many
other awards which are considered prestigious in my profession. But the greatest award I have ever received was that

check — my diploma — made out to Billy Joel in 1970. This particular check was enough to cover my rent and my expenses. It was also enough to convince me that I no longer needed to work in a factory or be a short-order cook or pump gas or paint houses or do any of the other day jobs I had done in order to make ends meet. That check meant that I was now able to make a living solely by doing the thing that I loved most — making music. It meant that I had become self-reliant as a musician. I will never forget that day. I consider it to be one of the most important days in my life.

I also remember the twenty-one-year-old Billy Joel and I often wonder what it would be like if we could, somehow, meet each other. Here I am, forty-two, exactly twice his age. What would I think of him? Would I find him to be naive, arrogant, simplistic, crude, noble, hopelessly idealistic? Perhaps all of these things. But more important, what would he think of me? Have I fulfilled his dream? Have I created the kind of music he would have wanted to have written? Have I compromised any of his ideals? Have I broken any of the promises I made to him? Have I lost the desire to be the best he could be? Would he be disappointed in me? Would he even like me?

That twenty-one-year-old has been the biggest pain in the neck I have had to endure in my life. Yet he has had more influence on the work I have done than anyone else for the last twenty-one years. He has been my greatest teacher, my deepest conscience, my toughest editor, and

my harshest critic. He has significantly shaped my life. I can say to you today that what you are at this moment in your lives you will always be in your hearts.

When I met with your fellow students, they asked me what is the most powerful lesson I have learned. After eleven years of classical training, I learned to play the piano, but I realized that I was not destined to be another Van Cliburn. I learned to write songs, although what I really wanted to write were symphonies like Beethoven. I have learned to perform, but somehow I knew I would never be able to move like Michael Jackson or sing like Ray Charles.

Out of respect for things that I was never destined to do, I have learned that my strengths are a result of my weaknesses, my success is due to my failures, and my style is directly related to my limitations. You see, the only original things I have ever done have been accidents, mistakes, flubs, foul-ups, and their attendant solutions. I have an inherent talent for stumbling onto something. I am an expert at making bad choices and illogical decisions. I have discovered that after all those years of musical instruction, after all that practice to be perfect, after all that hard work trying to compose the right notes, I am gifted with the knack of hitting exactly the wrong notes at precisely the right time.

This is the secret of originality. Think about it. You may have learned all there is to know about reproducing the art of someone else, but only you can commit a colossal blunder in your own exquisite style. This is what makes

you unique. But then you are faced with solving the problem. This is what makes you inventive. Commit enough blunders and you become an artist. Solve all the problems you have created and they will call you a genius.

I have learned that no matter how successful or proficient or accomplished I might think I am, I am always going to make mistakes. I will always have to face some difficulties. I am always going to have to deal with the possibility of failure, and I will always be able to utilize these things in my work. So I am no longer afraid of becoming lost, because the journey back always reveals to me something new about my life and about my own humanity, and that is, ultimately, good for the artist.

Now these same students also asked me if I set out to make it "to the top" or if I set out to be wealthy. If all I desired was wealth, then all I would have made was money. If all I set out to do was make it to the top, then all I would have been was Number One — a good number, but still only a number. What I set out to do was to be very good at what I do for my own satisfaction. As it turned out, being very good has a great deal of value to people, and that value in turn brought me to the top and also brought me financial success. But these things are merely by-products and not ends in themselves. I have derived much more happiness from making music than from making money; although, if I had taken a few courses in accounting, I might have derived more satisfaction as well as more money.

Since this is the 450th anniversary of the founding of the Jesuit order and the 500th birthday of St. Ignatius, in the spirit of the Jesuit ideal, you have chosen "service to the community and service to others" as your theme. This is an enlightened goal. I am celebrating the fiftieth birthday of Bob Dylan, and as Bob said, "You gotta serve somebody." Through my work, I have had the opportunity to travel the world and in doing so realized that I cannot save it — not the whole thing, anyway. But I have tried to protect and preserve a tiny little part of it. I have had the honor and privilege of using my good fortune to help others. I am not quite sure how one measures service. I am sure we would all like to do more. However, if you do what you can, when you can, and sometimes when you cannot, perhaps that is enough. I would ask you to understand that the greatest service you can do for others is to fulfill your own heart's desires and become the best you can be for yourselves. Even though you will fall down and foul up and make mistakes as I have — as everyone does — you will make this world a better place if you can bring to it your own unique and individual excellence and quality and originality. This is your gift to give. This is the greatest service you can render to your community and to others.

Before I wind this up, I would like to thank those same students for revealing to me one of life's small secrets. I have been traveling for twenty-five years and I have faced more junk food and hamburgers than most people I know.

I am sure that at one time or another, you have all been faced with trying to get ketchup out of a new bottle onto your junk food of choice. I never knew there was an easy way to get the ketchup out of the new bottle, but these students showed me how. For me this was one of life's small triumphs — a great mystery revealed. In sharing their secret with me, I know I will never have to dread the new ketchup bottle again. This might seem like a very small and trivial bit of information to share, but for me it meant a few less frustrating moments in my life. This is important to me. So please, do not ever misjudge the importance or relevance of what you know and what you have learned. It is important to someone, somewhere.

I hope that you all will appreciate small triumphs like this throughout your lives. I think you will find that great, historic feats are rare, but the joy of life is made up of obscure and seemingly mundane victories that give us our own small satisfactions, our own personal pleasures, and our own momentary revelations.

Thank you for inviting me here to speak today; I am very proud to accept the honor you are bestowing upon me. I will cherish this as I cherish the memory of that young musician getting his first decent paycheck twenty-one years ago. Welcome to the fire — now it is your turn to hold the hose.

Billy Joel

FLORENCE GRIFFITH JOYNER

Florence Griffith Joyner earned the title "World's Fastest Woman" with her world records in the 100- and 200-meter track events. In 1988, she became the first American woman ever to win four medals—three gold and one silver—in one Olympic year. Born in Los Angeles in 1959, Joyner began running at the age of six when she was challenged by her father to catch a jack rabbit. She founded and ran numerous organizations, along with co-chairing the President's Council on Physical Fitness and Sports. Joyner shared her many talents through fund-raising activities and continued to be sought after as a spokeswoman and talk show guest until her untimely death in 1998.

FLORENCE GRIFFITH JOYNER

The American University
Washington, D.C.
May 8, 1994

As you move forward from American University, I would like to offer you a few thoughts to carry on your journey.

I was born and raised in Watts, the seventh of eleven siblings. My mother instilled in her children the values of independence, individualism, and perseverance. She stressed the need to perform as best you can and served as my role model and inspiration. All of us need role models and inspiration in striving toward our goals. It is critical that you identify the right role models and are inspired by their words and deeds. I say this because we have all known those whose inspirational words were not matched by their deeds. If you are to be the future leaders of this country, you must lead not only through words but through action.

It is critical that you continually assess where you are in all facets of your life, determine where you want to go, and set goals that you wish to achieve. But remember, achieving your goals is not your destination, just part of your journey. As Oliver Wendell Holmes said, "The riders in a race do not stop short when they reach the goal. There is a little finishing canter before coming to a standstill. There is time to hear the kind voice of friends and to say

to one's self: 'The work is done.' But just as one says that, the answer comes: 'The race is over, but the work never is done while the power to work remains.'"

While you have worked hard, first to gain admittance to American University and then to fulfill all the requirements needed for graduation, your work is not done. While your goal to graduate is achieved, new goals must be established and work commenced to achieve those goals. This cycle will be repeated again and again in your lives, because the true challenge of life is to achieve one's goals and move on to new ones.

One of my goals was to represent our great country in the Olympics as a sprinter. I was fortunate enough to achieve that goal and won a silver medal in the 1984 Olympics. After that experience I immediately set a new goal to win a gold, and was most fortunate to win three gold medals in 1988. It has been said by countless authorities that at the world-class level, one is either a sprinter or a distance runner. One of my new goals is to disprove this theory and represent my country in the marathon in the 1996 Olympics.

Never has America's interest in health care been higher. Yet, at the heart of health care lies the responsibility of every individual to lead a healthy life, with physical activity at the core. In my role as cochair of the President's Council on Physical Fitness and Sports, my goal is to help all Americans recognize the benefits of physical activity

and adopt the exercise habit for life. I hope that the eight graduates who are here today receiving a M.A. in health fitness management play a pivotal role in that effort.

There is a final thought that I offer you. If you wish to leave this world better than when you found it, you must care about others. I started my running career under the auspices of the Sugar Ray Robinson Youth Foundation. I have tried to provide others with a similar experience through the Florence Griffith Joyner Foundation. The foundation provides youth with the necessary financial, emotional, and educational support in achieving their goals, promoting self-esteem and social interaction while involving family and friends in the process.

Mother Teresa once said that "We are not capable of accomplishing great things. We can only accomplish little things with great love." Just as winning an Olympic gold medal is really the culmination of thousands of "little" practice sessions, the true measure of your success will be how you achieved your goals while continually caring for others on thousands of "little" occasions and set the example for the next generation to emulate.

Florence Griffith Joyner

137

WILMA P. MANKILLER

In 1983, Wilma P. Mankiller was the first female to be elected deputy chief of the Cherokee Nation. In the historic 1987 election, she was the first female elected principal chief. As leader of one of the largest Native American tribes in the United States, she helped the Cherokee people achieve economic independence and renewed pride in their culture. She served as principal chief until 1995. Born in 1945 in Stilwell, Oklahoma, Mankiller gained an understanding of rural poverty early in life through personal experience. Today, she is instrumental in building self-esteem through community involvement within the Native American tribe. She has brought about significant changes including better education, health care, and improvements in adult literacy.

WILMA P. MANKILLER

Northern Arizona University
Flagstaff, Arizona
December 18, 1992

I ran into someone at the hotel this morning who asked me about how to address me on my credit card. It has "Wilma Mankiller, Principal Chief," and that is interesting because I think some people still have a little trouble identifying with a female principal chief. It reminded me of the first time I had to address this issue. I went to a very prestigious eastern college to do a panel on Indian economic development, and this young man picked me up at the airport to take me to the university. He asked me, "Since principal chief is a male term, how should I address you?" I just ignored him and looked out the window of the car, and then he asked me if he should address me as "Chieftains." I continued to look out the window, and then he thought he would get silly and cute. He asked me if he should address me as "Chiefette." I finally told him to address me as Ms. Chief — mischief. So we went out to the university, and this young man had the fortune or misfortune, I am not sure, to be one of the people who got to ask the panel questions. His question to me was about my last name.

Mankiller is my maiden name, and way back in

141

Cherokee history, Mankiller was like the "keeper of the village" — like the equivalent of a general or someone who watched over a village — and this one fellow liked the title so much he kept it as his name; but that's not what I told this young man. I told him it was a nickname and I had earned it. So somewhere back East there is a young man who is wondering what I did to earn my last name.

I am not going to give the standard advice about going out into the world, because many of you have already been out in the world and worked and been very involved in your communities. What I would like to do is encourage you in whatever you pursue or wherever you go from here to get involved. What I have seen, I think, in the United States, not just in my community or tribal community or rural community but in the United States in general, is a trend for all of us to think that somebody else is going to solve our problems for us.

It was interesting during this last year watching the presidential election and being aware of all these daunting sets of problems we face in this country — economy, education, health care, problems in the inner city; and everybody expecting somebody else to solve them. In the presidential election, no matter who was chosen for a candidate, people were counting on this one man to be able to articulate a clear vision for the future and then take care of all of the problems for the country. Do not think this is going to happen.

Even in my own community I have heard people

talk about the environment, housing, hopelessness, or any of the problems that we have; "Well, they're going to solve that problem." I see that also in American society it is always, "They're going to solve that problem." I don't know who "they" are. I always tell our own people that I don't know who they are referring to. To me the only people who are going to solve our problems are ourselves — people like you and me. We have got to personally take charge and solve our problems. I do not think that a great prophet is going to come along and save this country or save us and deal with all of these problems in a vacuum. We all have to take part in that. So I would encourage you to get involved; you will be immensely rewarded by getting into public service or by doing small things around your community and trying to help others.

The other advice I have to give you is, do not live your life safely. I would take risks and not do things just because everybody else does them. In my generation someone who had a big impact on me was Robert Kennedy, who in one speech said, "Some people see things the way they are and ask why, and others dream things that never were and ask why not?" I think that is where I hope many of you will be — people that question why things are and why we have to do them the way we have always done them. I hope you will take some risks, exert some real leadership on issues, and if you will, dance along the edge of the roof as you continue your life here.

Finally, I just want to make a couple of comments about where I see our country going in general. I just came back from the Economic Summit in Little Rock, Arkansas, which was an intense two-day session focusing specifically on how to stimulate the economy, both short term and long term. I was encouraged by the number and diversity of people there — Republicans and Democrats. People from every sector of the business community and every sector of society talking collectively about how to get the country moving again.

I think one of the things we have to do as a nation, besides addressing specific issues like the economy, health care, education, inner cities, and that sort of thing, is we have to examine the extent to which we continue to have stereotypes about one another. I think it is very difficult for us to collectively and symbolically join hands and begin to move forward in solving this country's problems if we continue to have these stereotypes about one another. There still exist in this country many negative stereotypes about black people, Latin people, and Asian people. God knows there are terrible stereotypes about Native Americans; these have to be overcome before we can move forward.

Sometimes I sit down with a diverse group of people in Oklahoma to work on some problem that we all have in common; it is almost like sitting down with people who have some kind of veil over their face or something. We all look at each other through this veil that causes us to

see each other through these stereotypes. I think we need to lift back the veil and deal with each other on a more human level in order to continue to progress.

The minority population in this country is dramatically increasing, and that is a fact. If we continue to have this increase in minority population, we need to find ways of dealing with each other and working with each other in much better ways, because it affects everybody. I do not think that we can say that what happens in Detroit does not somehow affect all America, because it does. I would urge all of you who are here today, both graduates and families, to examine the extent to which we hold those stereotypes about one another. And finally, I would hope my being here and spending just a couple of minutes today would help you to eliminate any stereotypes you might have about what a chief looks like.

RALPH NADER

Ralph Nader has been called America's most famous and most effective social critic. For nearly five decades, he has fought relentlessly as a consumer crusader and public defender. His concern and vision focuses on empowering citizens to create a government that responds to their needs. He has built an effective national network of citizen groups that has impacted areas ranging from tax reform to nuclear energy to health and safety programs. Founded in 1969, Nader's Washington-based network includes the Center for Study of Responsive Law, an organization for researching such subjects as food safety, pollution, and the Interstate Commerce Commission. Ralph Nader was born in 1934 in Winsted, Connecticut.

RALPH NADER

Harvard University
Cambridge, Massachusetts
June 3, 1981

At this time in your life, near the peak of your idealism and possibly as free to experiment, question, pioneer as you may ever be again, many of you may be ready to explore a work where you bring your conscience and time and talent altogether to work every day to improve your society. This is the meaning of citizenship. It may come as a surprise to some people to learn that citizen work makes possible traditional employment and much economic activity. Citizen work built a nation where rights, constitutional to contractual, make possible greater economic prosperity. Police states are almost never prosperous economies, no matter what their natural resource endowment may be. Monopoly capitalism never is much good for people and for equitable economic development. The history of Brazil is instructive on this point.

Citizen work produced the land grant colleges and the private colleges which provided multiple points of entry of millions of Americans seeking self-improvement and fulfillment. Citizen work enacted the Homestead Law in the 1860s, which gave 160 acres to individuals who worked them and thereby assured that much of the great-

est agricultural breadbasket of the world would not quickly become a collection of giant plantations. Instead, this law encouraged a spread of millions of small, productive farmers who loved their land and who, in turn, nourished the main political-economic reforms of the past century.

More recently, citizen work has been responsible for the principal advances in American justice. Four black freshmen engineering students with their now-historic sit-in at that North Carolina lunch counter twenty-one years ago were engaging in constitutionally protected citizen work. At least the Supreme Court of the United States thought so. Other citizens, individually and in groups, took on the silent violence of pollution and environmental wreckage from the lead-afflicted ghetto children to the poisonous spills in the air and water. Still others stood tall at their place of work to become ethical whistleblowers against corruption, crime, fraud, and waste. They were the trustees for millions of affected consumers, taxpayers, and workers.

These domestic patriots had everything material to lose and everything noble to win. What was that courageous impetus to their intellect that guided their actions? A sense of communion with the most widely shared value of humankind, a golden rule applied to their daily experience. The quality control inspector at General Motors who, after numerous reports to his foreman were ignored, put his job on the line in the mid-sixties by exposing risks of carbon monoxide leakage in the company's cars, was asked why he

did what he did. His reply was too simple for the reporters; it was the shop-floor version of the golden rule.

The opportunities for citizen work, on and off the job, have never been more demanding in a world where tragedy, peril, and risk are found side by side with brilliant but unused scientific, engineering, and organizational solutions. These opportunities beckon you. They invite all the skills, stamina, and creativity that you possess. No academic discipline is irrelevant. Problems to be resolved are like bodies of knowledge; they are a seamless web demanding the varied best that human minds have to offer. Over time a pollution crisis, for example, needs to draw on almost every discipline which your university embraces — from the physical sciences to the social sciences to the traditional professions and, yes, most definitely, to the humanities.

How, you may ask, after some sixteen years of an institutional education largely indifferent to learning about and engaging in citizen work — an education whose primary thrust flows from memorization to regurgitation to vegetation — can one acquire the desire? There is no single entrance. Try viewing these United States as an exporter of humane democratic examples. Try seeing citizen work not as a necessary chore but as a delight, a joy, a counterpoint to alienation, powerlessness, and boredom, a way to stretch your analytic and normative skills. Try etching out a future America where most citizens would feel a personal obligation to spend at least ten percent of their

time working on the problem or challenge of their choice in order to improve their community or world, where most citizens would reject the "what will be, will be" attitude of never fighting City Hall, nor Goliath, Incorporated, where most citizens would reject the facile cynicism of hating "the government" but would rather make it their government and their way of accomplishing community objectives.

These are self-actuating determinations; no laws, budgets, or elixirs are required. But, once actuated, solutions begin to be applied to what hitherto were seen as intractable problems. A functioning democracy permits people to always build power behind their quest for fair treatment and opportunity. It permits people to use directly the modern communications systems now controlled by a few firms. It permits people to shape the investment direction of more than a trillion dollars of pension funds and bank deposits, which they already own. People gaining control of the wealth that they already own for themselves or as trustees for their descendants — from the public airwaves to the public lands, from shares in companies to the pension funds — forge the link between responsible owners and a responsive political economy. Never have the separations between ownership and control, as illuminated in the early 1930s by Berle and Means, been so diverse, so pervasive throughout the economy, and so consequential for the future of economic and political democracy.

It is well to keep in mind that, unlike past genera-

tions, our generation worldwide has created two risks —
nuclear armaments and penetrating masses of pollution —
which could destroy life on earth. These two mounting
risks place a particularly strenuous set of moral imperatives
on our public-citizen roles.

So ask yourself: What kind of work would you
really like to do in life after Harvard, if money were no ob-
ject? Then start cranking in the dollars and see at what dollar level your ideal choice of work becomes overwhelmed
by your instrumental choice of work. From there, proceed
to adjust your available time so that you do not have either
to suffer your satisfaction or satisfy your suffering. There
are many hours in the day for diversifying your interests.
Whether you choose to develop consumer-side businesses
like cable TV co-ops or neighborhood-based legal, health,
or repair services, or whether you choose to enlarge or
build problem-solving civic groups, to suggest just two directions. Do keep in mind that the highest practice of citizenship is to defend the political rights of those who may
disagree with you as well as those who concur with your
pursuits. That is truly the golden rule of a democracy.

Congratulations to you, your parents, your teachers,
and to the country that is entitled to receive your wisest
contributions.

Ralph Nader

KATHERINE D. ORTEGA

Katherine Ortega served as the 38th treasurer of the United States from 1983 to 1989, following an impressive career in both the public and private sectors. Prior to her appointment to this position by President Reagan in 1982, Ortega was a bank executive and certified public accountant. She has served on numerous public and private committees, commissions, and boards, and was an alternate representative to the United Nations General Assembly. Born in New Mexico in 1934, Mrs. Ortega credits much of her success to her father's good example and verbal encouragement.

KATHERINE D. ORTEGA

Kean State College
Union, New Jersey
June 6, 1985

One of the requirements of every commencement speaker is that they offer some advice. Well, get ready, here it comes.

Soon you will be leaving the company of those who think they have all the answers — your professors, instructors, and counselors — and going out into what we like to call the real world. In time you will meet up with other people who think they have all the answers. These people are called bosses. My advice is: humor them.

A little later you will meet additional people who think they have all the answers. These are called spouses. My advice is: humor them, too.

And if all goes well, in a few years you will meet still another group of people who think they have all the answers. These are called children. Humor them.

Life will go on, your children will grow up, go to school, and someday they could be taking part in a commencement ceremony just like this one. And who knows, the speaker responsible for handing out good advice might be you. Halfway through your speech, the graduate sitting next to your daughter will lean over and ask, "Who is that woman up there who thinks she has all the answers?" Well,

thanks to the sound advice you are hearing today and that I hope you will all pass on, she will be able to say, "That is my mother. Humor her."

Let me begin by expressing my congratulations on all you have achieved, along with the gratitude I feel for your humoring me.

Some of you may well be wondering exactly what the treasurer of the United States is and what she does when not addressing graduating classes. A lot of people seem to get me confused with the secretary of the treasury. Or they think I print the money which the secretary spends. Or else they believe I spend all day at my desk in Washington personally signing all those dollar bills that come off the presses at the Bureau of Engraving and Printing.

Perhaps one or more of you might go on from this bright occasion to another place in the sun. Perhaps one day your name might be affixed to our country's currency. Or perhaps it will appear on bills introduced in Congress. Who knows? Perhaps it will show up at the bottom of a legislative page in the space reserved for the presidential signature. After all, it was one of this state's great governors who went on to become one of this nation's greatest presidents. His name was Woodrow Wilson, and it was he who once declared that "We should not only use all the brains we have, but all that we can borrow."

Think about that for a moment and place it within the context of your education here at Kean. It is tempting,

amidst the day's confusion, the popping flashbulbs and tearful good-byes, to think you have lost something very special. It is all too easy to think of this ceremony as the end of a happy time. It is just as easy to shrink from the uncertainties and risks of whatever it is that lies beyond this field. Perhaps that real world of ours is really as cold and forbidding a place as it looks on the network news or in the morning paper. Maybe no diploma can overcome the small, nagging fear that this is one threshold you cross at your own peril.

I am sure there are some among you today who think you are inheriting a highly uncertain world, a world burdened by armaments and a world ravaged by hunger, a world long on hypocrisy and short on opportunity. The world is an imperfect place. You do not need me to tell you that. But the world is also a perfectible place. If I did not believe that, I would not be here.

Now where, you are no doubt asking yourselves, did she ever come up with that idea? Well, let me tell you. When I was a girl, the youngest of nine children, I lived amidst the white sands and lunar landscape of New Mexico. When I was about your age, I hoped to become a schoolteacher. But I was told not to bother. Why? Because in eastern New Mexico, the part of the state where the best-paying jobs were to be found, employers simply did not believe in hiring Hispanics. But times have changed. They hire Hispanics now. More than a few Hispanics are themselves doing the hiring.

When I was a girl, my brothers wore tattered blue jeans long before they became fashionable attire. They sold perfume door-to-door to put bread on the Ortega family table. My father augmented his own income by nailing together custom-made coffins. The one thing he refused to bury was his unshakable conviction that each life is special, and that each one's calling was important not for the income it generated but the character it called forth. He dismissed both bloodlines and bank accounts as insignificant. He had contempt only for those who put on airs. "Get that chip off your shoulder," he used to say to us. "You are as good as anyone else." Then he said something to me, something in its own way as educational and as liberating as anything ever taught in a formal classroom. "If you are going to work for someone," he said, "give it the full eight hours plus. If you are going to do it at all, do it right."

These are the words that propelled me into the world of business and banking. Similar words, no doubt, have accompanied each of you on your way through Kean State. Do not ever forget them. Not for a moment. Because they are your ticket of admission to an America closer than ever before to the nation dreamed of by her founders. A country that is colorblind, a republic without walls. A nation which can ill afford to dispense with any of those brains Woodrow Wilson long ago urged it to borrow.

Think for a moment about the accelerating pace of

change in all our lives. Then think about the implications of change. Times of change are times of challenge, now more than ever. But take it from me, as one who has seen much change in her own life, these are the challenges which test our talents and forge our abilities. Someone who is seventy years old in 1985 has lived through a period of more change than in all of previously recorded history. He has witnessed the birth of radio and television, the advent of mass transportation, the transformation from a rural to an urban society. He has become a citizen of the Atomic Age, when mankind itself clings to a narrow window ledge, uncertain which way to go, yet convinced he must take some step toward controlling the weapons of death which now deface our planet. In a single lifetime, that seventy-year-old has seen much to disturb him but more to encourage him. He has seen the role of women recast. Gone are the days of Rosie the Riveter. Fast disappearing are those "firsts" — role models who broke a path, and who were placed on a pedestal by a society unwilling to see them become the rule.

In our own time, we have seen one barrier after another fall before the forces of conscience. In the short span of personal memory, freedom has been distributed more evenly. I know, for my own life provides testimony to the fact. I harbor a fierce loyalty to this doctrine of human possibility, having lived through wars and survived the bleak Depression, having encountered prejudice and closed

doors — but also warm support and open arms. Today the world is your oyster. However, your focus should be on the pearl inside the oyster. How is it created? It is created when a grain of sand gets inside the shell, irritating the creature within and forcing it to spin a luminous shell within a shell. In other words, an example of creative tension within nature. In the years to come, your years, there will be plenty of creative tension. In a world full of lasers and fiber optics, we will need to rely on people like yourselves to ward off a depersonalized society. In my own profession, automatic teller machines may be efficient, but they are no substitute for human beings. In those same years, freedom will require you to defend it, to purify it, to extend it to every man, woman, and child, in the neighborhoods of Newark and the rich acres which together make this America's Garden State. We will have to find ways to expand our economy so as to include all those previously abandoned to the outskirts of hope. At the same time, we will need to preserve our environment, which is our most precious legacy to generations yet unborn. The years ahead loom before us at times when nothing is certain, except uncertainty.

You have been well prepared to deal with the world of tomorrow. Here at Kean State you have sampled two educations — one in the classroom and another you have given yourself. Here you have discovered that so long as books are kept open, then minds can never be closed. You have been grounded in timeless values. Yet you have also

been trained to flourish in a world awash in change. Put those changes to work for you, and you will make more than a living. You will make history.

Only one thing is changeless, and that is my faith in the individual. My belief that one man or one woman can make a profound difference. My father made such a difference by his example and his verbal encouragement. I have tried to make a difference, through self-application and sharing whatever lessons I have learned with others who seek to add their talents to the mainstream of America's economic and social life. So can you, fortified by faith in God and faith in freedom, faith in the essential goodness of the human race and faith in your own destinies. My graduation promised no instant solutions and no permanent prosperity — only the opportunity to try to achieve these things. It did not banish struggle. On the contrary, it opened a new chapter in a lifelong struggle.

For over the years I have learned that life is a voyage of discovery and not a safe harbor. It is on the voyage that we learn how to steer our own lives and with them the life of the nation we love. We learn to coexist with our fears, to surmount the obstacles before us. We find ways to defy danger, even as we reach deep within ourselves for solutions to the challenges of the age. Today, you lay claim to the future. You take a step — nothing more, nothing less — toward making that future your own. But what a step! And what a future beckons. Remember the pearl inside the

oyster. Remember the lessons imparted here. Most of all, remember and revere the investment of love made over many years by parents, teachers, and friends — all of them handing you the baton and wishing you well in the ongoing race of life.

"We should not only use all the brains we have, but all that we can borrow."

In a world marked by economic and political competition, in an age filled with scientific wonders and genetic marvels, in a globe where national boundaries are no longer confused with natural barriers to commerce and culture, brains are the most important commodity we have. We need you, now and for as long as you are willing to participate in the great pageant of your times. Join those times, and you can make them reflect your own priorities. You can make America all she was meant to be. You can realize your faith, and in so doing, renew our hold on the planet. Be bold. Be brave. Most of all, believe in yourselves and your capacity to shape the world of tomorrow, which begins today. May God go with you, and may His light show you the way for all the years to come.

Katherine D. Ortega

GENERAL COLIN L. POWELL

Born in New York City in 1937 and raised in the South Bronx, General Colin Powell was the first African-American and the youngest man ever to serve as the Chairman of the Joint Chiefs of Staff. Best known to the American public for his firm and decisive handling of the 1991 Persian Gulf War, he was responsible for advising the President and planning all land, sea, and air campaigns. Powell retired from his position as Chairman of the Joint Chiefs of Staff in late 1993 but continues to be a sought-after speaker. Currently, he serves on the boards of several non-profit organizations and is Chairman of America's Promise, an organization dedicated to the advancement of the nation's youth.

GENERAL COLIN L. POWELL

United States Military Academy
West Point, New York
May 31, 1990

It is impossible for me to attend a commissioning ceremony without my thoughts drifting back to my own commissioning thirty-two years ago next week.

Although you and I are separated by more than a generation in age and an epoch in terms of the world you are entering compared to the one I did, I suspect the old Second Lieutenant Powell standing there and the new Second Lieutenant Powell sitting out there have more in common than you might expect.

First of all, an overwhelming sense of accomplishment in meeting the challenge that was set before us. The satisfaction of work well done.

I'm sure there is also a feeling of excitement as you anticipate the future, leaving the world you have known here at West Point for the world you will discover in your first assignment.

We share the same pride of following in the footsteps of countless others who went before us and who dedicated their lives to preserving our nation's heritage.

And, of course, we both share beaming parents and

167

family smiling on with a mixture of pride, surprise, and in some cases outright disbelief.

And, finally, without question we share the intense desire for the speech to end and for the party to begin.

If our experiences on the day we received our commissions are similar, the world today is far different than when I began my military career. Let me take you back thirty-two years and tell you a little about the world I entered.

My first tour was overseas in Germany as a second lieutenant in charge of forty infantrymen guarding a place called the Fulda Gap, on the massively armed border between East and West Germany. The year was 1958.

NATO was less than a decade old. West Germany had been in the alliance less than three years. Two years earlier the Soviets had poured 200,000 troops and 4,000 tanks into Hungary to stamp out the dreams of the Hungarian people for freedom.

The Berlin Wall had not yet been built. One year earlier the Soviets had launched Sputnik, shattering our notions of intellectual superiority and ushering in a period of missile-rattling diplomacy on the part of Premier Khrushchev that culminated in the Cuban missile crisis.

One month after I arrived in Germany, Premier Khrushchev announced that the Soviet Union was committed to putting an end not only to the Western presence

in Berlin but in all of Germany. None of us knew if war might be imminent. It was a troubled time.

And now, today, the world you inherit is quite different. It is a world fundamentally reshaped by the revolution of 1989.

The Berlin Wall, symbol of oppression, is down and now being broken up by the East Germans to sell as souvenirs.

In Czechoslovakia, a playwright is now president.

In Poland, a shipyard worker has welded the idea of freedom onto the mast of the new Polish Republic.

The menacing Red Army I have watched for thirty-two years, designed to sweep westward, is retreating as the forces of democracy sweep eastward.

The prospect of a world war is no longer a fear. The world is still troubled, but the prospect of peace is now more than a dream.

And what of Fulda, where I started? It's still there, waiting for one of you. But by the time you get there it may not be an armed border camp. It may well be a place inside a now-unified Germany, where you will be insuring the peace rather than deterring a war.

And when next I visit Fulda, I'll reminisce with the German farmers who still bring hot coffee to young American lieutenants on cold winter days.

Our nation has won two great victories in my life-

time. One on the battlefield forty-five years ago; the other without firing a single shot in combat.

In the first victory we defeated fascism by the force of our arms; in the second we defeated communism by the strength of our arms. In both conflicts our democratic system of values made the difference.

At the end of the first conflict, General Omar Bradley, who was to become the first Chairman of the Joint Chiefs of Staff, spoke from where I am speaking now. He looked back on the sacrifices and the bloodshed, the pain and the triumph.

He thought of D-Day, when we began our mission of liberating Europe. And he said, ". . . this was not an army, not a navy, but a nation sailing to war. Our ships were filled with the achievements and hopes of the American people."

Today, I stand before you at the threshold of our second victory. In this second struggle we had no D-Days. There were no great naval battles, no invasions, no grand armies sweeping across a continent devastated by tyranny.

But in this second struggle we, too, were filled with the achievements and hopes of the American people. We, too, stood at the outposts of liberty. We, too, paid the price, we showed resolve, we showed the will of free people united, and we prevailed.

We Americans are a pragmatic people. When we set out to meet the Soviet challenge, our goal was not to

achieve worldwide domination but to make it clear to all that we would never acquiesce in the destruction of all that was dear to us and to our friends and our allies.

In this struggle, our institutions sustained us, our values nurtured us, and our armed forces protected us. In this struggle we were not alone. We were joined by allies who shared our belief that peace and security cannot be obtained at the expense of freedom.

In 1945, Clark Clifford, one of President Truman's closest advisors, wrote to the President telling him what needed to be done to meet the Soviet challenge. He said we had to make the Soviets change their minds. Instead of thinking that war was inevitable, we wanted them to join us in settling our differences peacefully. Clifford's hope was that the Soviets would come around when he said, "They realize that we are too strong to be defeated and too determined to be frightened."

Today, under President Gorbachev we see dramatic changes that bear out the wisdom of Clifford's advice.

Today, at this hour, President Gorbachev is in Washington meeting with President Bush to continue their efforts to fundamentally reshape our relations in the way we have prayed for, worked for, and stood guard for.

Today, President Gorbachev is here because he has taken a measure of our strength and the challenges facing his own people: a people striving to come to terms with their past, to reform their present, and to plan for their future.

Who among us even a year ago could have imagined that today the Soviets would be implementing controlled market policies or that in the Russian Republic an opposition leader would be voted in after a raucous election campaign with all the earthiness of a Chicago primary.

The way of the future is clearly democracy. Why? Because it works. That's why it is sweeping Eastern Europe. But it goes beyond Europe. It is light reaching into the darkest corners of oppression in the world. It works. It works because it frees the human mind and the human soul to reach their full potential.

And so we are at a watershed in our history. Strength, determination, resolve — all in service of our ideals. It is the coming together of American power and American purpose. It worked in 1945. It worked in the revolution of 1989. It works today and will work tomorrow. In our struggles we have learned a valuable lesson: in a democracy, power without purpose is morally unsustainable; purpose without power is militarily indefensible.

On the threshold of our first great victory, General Bradley looked to the future. He looked to a time when our citizen army would no longer be engaged in combat but had to remain ready to defend our interests.

Bradley wanted a foundation stone of military strength to preserve and insure the peace. We know what happened to General Bradley's request. One year after our victory over aggression, our armed forces were a shell.

In blind hope that they will not be needed again, let us not repeat the mistake of the past by dismantling our armed forces when danger seems to be gone. That will not serve the long-term interests of the United States or our friends throughout the world. We must maintain a strong defense to maintain a strong America.

The language of my generation — Cold War, confrontation, containment — is disappearing in the wake of revolutionary change. But revolutions do not blot out history. Our task, therefore, is straightforward. We must recognize what has changed and what has not. We must identify what threats have receded and which have not. We must also remember what is constant, what endures.

The first enduring reality we must face is the Soviet Union itself. President Gorbachev has not embarked on his breathtaking revolution to relegate the Soviet Union to the status of a second-ranked power. Nor should we expect him to. I believe he is as sincere in wanting to reform his country as he is in making sure it continues to play a dominant role in world affairs.

Gennady Gerasimov, the Soviet spokesman at their Ministry of Foreign Affairs, spoke recently to a group of American college graduates. He outlined a litany of Soviet failures, all in service to an ideology which he said just didn't work. It was a remarkable admission. But he ended his talk by saying, "But we haven't done everything wrong, there are some things we have done right." And what

topped his list of Soviet successes? Nuclear weapons. Military power. He reminded his listeners, "We are a military superpower."

The Soviets are withdrawing their forces from Eastern Europe. But they will still maintain the largest, most modern military force on the Eurasian landmass.

Neither will the Soviets dismantle their impressive and modern nuclear arsenal. Whatever the outcome of Mr. Gorbachev's revolution, one fact remains: the Soviet Union will still possess thousands of nuclear warheads that can destroy America in thirty minutes. We must never allow ourselves to be at a nuclear disadvantage.

The Soviet threat has receded. And that is good. But the Soviet Union is a country that has demonstrated throughout its history that it will pay the price to remain a great power. That is the enduring reality behind the Soviet revolution today. And so while we applaud the Soviet revolution, let us not lose sight of the enduring reality of Soviet military power.

There is a second enduring reality, one that lies across the ocean in Europe. We are and will remain an Atlantic power, tied to Europe politically, economically, militarily, and culturally. This is accepted on both sides of the Atlantic. Shared values brought the U.S. and Europe together for collective defense. Unlike the Soviet Union, we did not impose an ideology on clients. We shared a heritage with allies. That is why none of our allies and friends across

the Atlantic wish us to disengage from the future evolution of Europe. And that is why we must remain in Europe.

A third enduring reality lies across that other great ocean, the Pacific. While we kept the peace in Europe for forty years we fought two bloody wars in Asia. When I was not defending collective security in Europe, I was fighting in Vietnam or standing guard in Korea. Today, few nations in Asia wish us ill will. To the contrary, our presence is viewed as a bulwark of stability in an area of the globe inhabited by a third of humanity. We must not shrink from our Pacific responsibilities.

And finally, a fourth enduring reality; one that highlights not how far we have traveled in the course of history, but how much further still we have to go. War, fundamentalism, drugs, and terrorism are all still with us. They were not spawned by communism's birth; they will not end with communism's demise.

In the Middle East, regimes have scarred Isaiah's prophecy and are beating their swords into missiles. In Central America, we had to call upon our citizen army to overthrow a despot and return Panama to its people.

Sixty years ago a treaty was signed declaring war to be an illegal instrument of diplomacy. Fifty million casualties later we understand that good intentions and declarations alone will not suffice to ensure the peace. Ready armed forces are the answer for the crisis no one ever expects.

We will remain joined together with our friends and allies; united by the common bonds of values and interests. We will do what is required of us to support the peace. American power and American leadership are still essential. We are a superpower. We must lead as a superpower. We must retain the strength of a superpower.

A strong, trained, ready, and proud American Army is the key to our continuing superpower strength. An Army sure of its roots. An Army proud of its past. An Army unafraid of the challenges of the future. An Army that will be as needed in the future as it has been in the past. An Army to insure the peace and to protect the nation against risk and uncertainty.

An Army that will be smaller but with each passing year will be better. An American Army deserving of the very best soldiers and leaders the nation can provide.

What you are about to enter is the finest peacetime American Army we have ever had.

I want to strike a bargain with you. Let the old General Powell worry about the defense budgets, peace dividends, and geopolitical trends. The young Lieutenant Powells, the ones out there today, you go and do what West Point second lieutenants have been doing since 1802 — lead your soldiers. Keep them fit and hardy, trained and ready. Keep them proud.

You and your soldiers are the guardians of the nation. You are the nation's life insurance. The American

people understand this and appreciate your service and commitment. They know the world is still a place of turmoil and danger.

Two hundred years ago, as the Constitution was being debated, one of its drafters suggested a numerical limit of 2,000 troops on the U.S. Army. George Washington agreed. "An excellent idea — if only we can convince our collected enemies to maintain no more than an equivalent amount."

Did Washington have a keen appreciation of imminent danger to the fledgling republic? Or did he appreciate that the clash between good and evil, between conflicting interests or competing ideologies, makes it dangerous to impose limits so arbitrary as to deny the U.S. the wherewithal to defend itself and its values?

Washington understood what it took: sentinels at the outposts of liberty. The enemy is incidental. The sentinel — well trained and ready — is not.

You and your soldiers will be those sentinels. You will be the ones on whose shoulders fall the responsibility for taking our Army, training it, nurturing it, preparing it for war, even as we seek the promise of an unprecedented peace.

Words like "leadership," "resolve," and "determination" are just words until they are brought to life by men and women who dedicate themselves to the profession of arms and the security and well-being of the nation. This is

as true today as it was in 1802 when this academy opened its doors for the first time.

General Bradley spoke of a nation sailing to war. We are a nation sailing toward peace — a peace that offers us more hope for security than at any time over the last half century. We will need our values to guide us, our elected officials to lead us, and our men and women in uniform to protect us.

And so as you leave here today, be strengthened by the 188 years of heritage that is now passed on to you by the "Long Gray Line." Remember the beauty and strength of this place and let it always be an inspiration to you. Remember the solid, gray granite of these walls and how these stones have stood against countless seasons, a symbol of America's strength around the crucible of her military leadership. And remember this simple charge — love your soldiers with all your heart and soul and mind and body. And selflessly serve your grateful nation.

CARL SAGAN

Carl Sagan was one of the nation's best-known astronomers. He was also an educator, author, and theorist, whose skill in communicating technical information to the general public enhanced our understanding of planetary surfaces and atmospheres, the earth's origins, and extraterrestrial life. Born in 1934 in New York City, he served as the David Duncan Professor of Astronomy and Planetary Sciences at Cornell until his untimely death in 1996. Dr. Sagan authored many articles and books, including the Pulitzer Prize-winning *The Dragons of Eden*, as well as seven other *New York Times* bestsellers. He co-wrote and hosted the public television series *Cosmos*, which brought the mystery of the universe home to many audiences.

CARL SAGAN

Wheaton College
Norton, Massachusetts
May 22, 1993

Humans have always had rites of passage for critical, transitional moments in our life histories. This is a tradition going back not just hundreds or thousands of years, but millions.

Our genus, the genus *Homo*, is a few million years old. Our species, *Homo sapiens*, is a few hundred thousand years old. We arose in the savannahs of East Africa. We were hunters and gatherers: no fixed abode, no property. We followed the game. Our numbers were few. Our powers were feeble. But we had technology.

We humans have been technologists from the beginning. It is true that the early technology was stone tools — and fire — a technology, incidentally, that we still have not entirely mastered. If you look in the paleoanthropological record in East Africa, you can find that different places have different stone-hewing traditions. We can tell from how the axes and other tools have been flaked and hewn that they taught these skills one way in one spot and a thousand kilometers away in quite a different way.

So that immediately means there had to be schools. And there had to be instruction. There had to be tests. There probably were failing grades. There probably was a

disgusted throwing away of ineptly manufactured tools. And there probably were graduation ceremonies, in which the elders stood around and congratulated those of both sexes who had succeeded in mastering the technology and the knowledge necessary for the future.

Today, there are nearly five and a half billion of us. We are all over the planet, even on the ocean floor and a couple of hundred miles up in space now and again. Our technology has given us formidable, maybe even awesome, powers. This technology is both our opportunity and our danger. It is a double-edged sword, just as fire was from the beginning.

We owe our lives — not just the quality of our lives, but the existence of our lives — to technology. Most people on earth would be dead if not for modern agriculture and modern medicine. At the same time, that technology permits weapons of mass destruction, permits inadvertent changes in the environment that sustains us all.

Clearly, before us is the very dicey job of using these enormous powers wisely. This is something that we have not had much experience in, because we have never had powers this great. The capability both for good and for evil is unexcelled. And that means that this generation — you young women and men — has an absolutely key role to play in the long adventure of the human species.

We are very close relatives to chimpanzees. We share 99.6 percent of our active genes with chimpanzees, which

means there is a lot about us we can learn from chimps. Now it is clear that chimp society is — how shall I say? — testosterone ridden. By no means all, but a great deal of the aggression and intimidation is something the males feel especially comfortable and happy with.

In times of stress and crowding, there is something very interesting that happens. This is brought out, for example, in the Arnhem colony of chimps in the Netherlands. The males, when they get annoyed, use rocks and stones; they like to throw things. The females are not into missiles. In times of crisis the males can be seen gathering lots of stones — their arms full, their fists clenched — to carry over and throw at their adversaries. The females walk over to these stone-laden males and pry their fingers open, take the stones out, and deposit them on the ground. Sometimes the males get huffy and regather the stones, whereupon the females do it again — sometimes three, four times — until the males get the point.

I have a feeling that the hereditary predisposition for females as meditators and peacemakers is in the 99.6 percent of the genes that we share with the chimps. And that leads me to wonder what the world would be like if women played a role proportionate to their numbers. I do not mean just the occasional woman prime minister who beats the boys at their own game. I mean real, proportionate sharing of power. I mean half, not a few percent, of the members of the Senate — women. I mean half, not zero,

of the succession of presidents being women. I mean half of the Joint Chiefs of Staff as women. I mean half the chief executive officers of major corporations as women.

Maybe it would change nothing. Maybe under these circumstances the institutions predetermine human behavior, and it does not matter whether you are a male or a female. But I like to think that is not the case, that in a world in which women truly share power, we would have a more just, more humane, and more hopeful future. Maybe this is just a pipe dream. But it is a kind of fantasy that I could not help but have in thinking about this class.

You have been given, in your four years here, some of the tools to preserve and, where necessary, to change the society and the global civilization. No one says this is easy. There are enormous forces of inertia and resistance to any change at all. And there are those who benefit and prosper from there being no change. Nevertheless, it is clear that our civilization is in trouble, that the current way we do things is not going to get us out of trouble, that significant changes are necessary. I hope you will make them.

One of the most important tools is skeptical or critical thinking. Put another way, equip yourself with a baloney-detection kit. Because there is an enormous amount of baloney that has to be winnowed out before the few shining gems of truth and reality can be glimpsed. And a lot of that baloney is proffered by those in power. That is their

job. Part of the job of education is to be able to tell what is baloney and what is not.

The urgency you feel to make change is just the extent that change will be made. Do not sit this one out. Do not play it safe. Understand the world and change it where it needs to be changed. Where it does not need it, leave it alone. Make our society better. Make a world worthy of the children that your generation will bear.

JONAS SALK, M.D.

Jonas Salk, a research scientist, gained his greatest recognition for developing the first effective polio vaccine. The vaccine helped save thousands of lives from a crippling disease that caused panic when it became an epidemic in the 1950's. Born in New York City in 1914, he served as a distinguished professor in international health sciences. In 1963, he became a founding director of the Jonas Salk Institute for Biological Studies in La Jolla, California. The institute developed into a progressive center for medical and scientific research. There he was engaged in the studies of the prevention and treatment of immune diseases, cancer, and the AIDS virus until his death in 1995.

JONAS SALK

Harvard University Medical School
Boston, Massachusetts
June 6, 1991

As I reflect upon the state of the art and science of medicine on the occasion of the commencement of your careers, as compared to the beginning of my life's work fifty-two years ago, I am in awe as I cast a glance into your next half century. I say your next half century because, when all is said and done, it becomes self-evident that our past, as will be true of the future, has been shaped by the expanding dimensions of the human mind.

One might well ask, what were the challenges of my generation, and what will be the challenges of yours? What will be different and what will be the same? Just as each age is golden in a different way, each generation has the opportunity to make of it what it will.

It would hardly be fitting at this moment to do more than suggest an attitude, a way to approach your future as physicians and scientists who will deal with human health and well-being. As I have observed what has been happening over time, it is evident that we have come a long way in controlling disease through our understanding of the biological dimensions. We are now in need of understanding the human dimensions as well.

When I speak of the human dimensions, I am thinking of the self that lies within the nucleus of the human atom, with its quantum of desire and its telos, or purpose, which is expressed in the ability to choose and assume responsibility, and in so doing, to survive and evolve as individuals and as a species.

It is clear that each of us has particular affinities sensed intuitively through our feelings of satisfaction as well as through the effects produced by our actions and the successes achieved. We need to follow our inclinations in this regard.

Over the course of a lifetime, it is the role played by our individual purpose and sense of responsibility, as displayed by the choices we make, that evokes the potential that we possess. In making these choices we will, hopefully, each in our own way, become examples that others may follow. In this regard, each of us is born to contribute in a different way.

Looking at my own life, I can see how desire and a sense of responsibility have allowed me to channel my own career. When my responsibilities for the initial work on vaccination against polio were completed, I was asked by Alan Gregg of the Rockefeller Foundation what I would do next. Before I could reply, he interjected, "Whatever you choose, do that which makes your heart leap." This comes to mind as I contemplate the transitions that you

now face and will continue to face as you progress through the stages of your lives.

While I would give you the same advice today, I have also learned that there are two great tragedies in life: to not get what you want and to get what you want. It was because I was denied my desire to pursue studies on rheumatic diseases during an elective period in medical school that I found myself in a laboratory concerned with studies on influenza. Ultimately this opportunity, which was not my preferred choice, proved to be of even greater good fortune, because it broadened my experiences so that I would be able to direct my career and assume the responsibility to meet the needs of my time.

I had always intended to engage in research, and I accepted an opportunity to leave my class at the end of the first year to become a research fellow in biochemistry. At the end of that year I had an opportunity to continue in the field of biochemistry. However, I chose to remain in medicine rather than be limited to a field of science only remotely related to matters of medical and human interest. Later, after my internship, I had an opportunity to become a surgeon. But I declined, preferring a career in laboratory and clinical research to continue my interest in what was later to be called vaccinology, a science that I sought to develop from the art that it had been at that time.

The challenges I chose were also defined by the

needs of the time. As a child I had observed the tragic consequences of the 1916 epidemic of poliomyelitis in New York City and the 1918 pandemic of influenza. While I do not recall being influenced by these experiences in a conscious way, the need to control these infectious diseases was apparent. It seemed natural, therefore, for me to choose this ripe and fruitful field in which to work.

After the work on influenza and polio, and in the course of exploratory studies on immunotherapy of cancer and of autoimmune disease, I saw the need for fundamental studies required to address clinically applicable ways to control such diseases. The value of combining the fundamental and clinical approaches is evident in my current interest in the prospects for immunotherapy and immunoprophylaxis of HIV infection.

I also began to appreciate the human side of nature and of science. It was with this in mind that the Institute for Biological Studies was created to deal with the human as well as the biological dimensions in health and disease.

My continuing interest in the human side of nature is why I chose to address some of the broader questions concerning the evolution of human health and disease in our time, rather than to practice clinical medicine, involving individual patients. I had a desire to serve as a physican to humankind, in whatever way this might be done. Drawn to certain questions I chose to ask, I found that I, too, was chosen by the opportunities afforded by having been in the

right place at the right time. Whatever the dynamics, they depended upon human qualities, one of which is a sense of responsibility.

Fifty-two years later, as I pursue my interest in the prospects for immunotherapy and immunoprophylaxis of HIV infection, it continues to be evident to me that the choices I have made have been out of this sense of responsibility.

And so it would seem that each of us has an opportunity to play a far more important role than may be apparent at first glance, and to do so individually as well as collectively, and not to leave such matters to others or to chance alone.

It may be up to the professions — perhaps influenced by the most interested physicians and scientists, given our instinct for healing — to begin to address the needs of the person, of the relationship of person to person, and of the person to and within society.

Who else, by profession and commitment, are better prepared to assume their share of responsibility for the future of the current generation and the generations that are to follow? We are speaking about our children, and our children's children, and all of the future generations for whom they, too, will be responsible. Not only will we have to care for many more individuals, with all the diversity that this implies, but also we will have to care for and maintain the health of more human gray matter than ever before.

In this regard, I have the sense that our humanity is being tested for our ability to deal with the morbidity and mortality for which we are the pathogens, acting both upon ourselves and others. In what way is this attributable to nature and in what way to nurture? How can such a question be addressed?

What we can say is that such behavior is, in effect, a product of evolution, with diversity seen not only in the different cultures and societies in the world but in our own culture and society as well. Rather than despair about what this implies and about all that remains to be achieved in this realm, I see hope. I sense in many whose careers have commenced in recent years a continuing interest and zeal to improve the quality of human life in all of its many dimensions. And I hear it reiterated here by you.

Hopefully the instinct for improving the human condition will prevail, and the wisdom needed to put to use the knowledge that we already possess will be brought to bear. It should be evident, from this perspective, that the challenges of the past were simple as compared to those with which we are now confronted.

It will be through our sense of responsibility, not only for the needs of our patients, but in a larger sense, for the health and well-being of humankind, that these challenges can be met. There is a need for physicians, scientists, and others who have concern for human life to work

194

together toward improving health and well-being in all of its dimensions. If we do not, who will be to blame for the future, to which we and our ancestors will have contributed? How will we be looked back upon by those who follow?

There is a need for each generation to set its own goals, its own hopes and purposes. Through the acceptance of responsibility to take the initiative, each generation creates the possibility for a better today and an even better tomorrow. Through the strength and power of hope, a sense of responsibility can be made operative. Therefore, there is a need to expand the number of those with these concerns from the few to the many, and to do so by example. It will be through the process of self-selection that the like-minded will come together to form natural relationships to change the quality of life, their own and the lives of those with whom they come into contact. There can be a more positive vision, a more hopeful vision, through assumption of this responsibility.

You come upon the scene at an important and meaningful moment in human history — I might even say, human evolution. You and those who follow will carry a greater burden, not only in the practice of your profession, but to help others see what you see, to know what you know, and to do what wisdom dictates for the maintenance and enhancement of human health and well-being.

This will require those with courage to take responsibility for the initiative needed to implement the realization of the visions you have. In this way, you will go far toward the ultimate that can be reasonably achieved, and in the process you will be amply rewarded for a job well done by the opportunity to do more.

Yours, Salk

DR. SEUSS

Dr. Seuss, the pen name for Theodor Seuss Geisel, is the author and illustrator of dozens of nonsense fantasies in verse. Among his most popular books are *The Cat in the Hat, Green Eggs and Ham, Horton Hatches the Egg, Hop on Pop,* and *How the Grinch Stole Christmas.* Born in Springfield, Massachusetts in 1904, he always had a talent for writing and drawing cartoons. After college, he found a career in advertising illustration. When the job was slow, he wrote *And to Think That I Saw It on Mulberry Street,* his first children's book. The reviews were so good and he had so many ideas, he never stopped creating! While Theodor Seuss Geisel died in 1991, Dr. Seuss lives on in the hearts of millions of adults and children.

DR. SEUSS

Lake Forest College
Lake Forest, Illinois
June 4, 1977

"MY UNCLE TERWILLIGER ON THE ART OF EATING POPOVERS"

My uncle ordered popovers
from the restaurant's bill of fare,
and, when they were served, he regarded them
with a penetrating stare. . . .
Then he spoke great Words of Wisdom
as he sat there on that chair:
"To eat these things," said my uncle,
"You must exercise great care.
You may swallow down what's solid . . .
BUT . . . you must spit out the air!"

And . . . as you partake of the world's bill of fare,
that's darned good advice to follow.
Do a lot of spitting out the hot air.
And be careful what you swallow.

Dr. Seuss

NEIL SIMON

Neil Simon's enormous popularity and success as a playwright and screenwriter comes from writing honestly about people and their relationships through the use of comedy. His Broadway hits include *Lost in Yonkers,* for which he won a Pulitzer Prize, *Brighton Beach Memoirs, Biloxi Blues, Broadway Bound, The Odd Couple* and *Sweet Charity.* His artistic talents have garnered him both Emmy and Tony Awards, and his plays, numbering more than thirty, have frequently won "Best Play" of the year. Recent autobiographical books include the first, *Neil Simon Rewrites: A Memoir,* and a second, *The Play Goes On.* Simon was born in 1927 in New York City and is the only living playwright for whom a Broadway theater is named.

NEIL SIMON

Williams College
Williamstown, Massachusetts
June 3, 1984

Mr. President, faculty, graduates, family, friends, squirrels, chairs, grass, statues, dormitories, campus, packed valises, tied-up books, lost sneakers, unreturned tennis rackets, tear-stained phonebooks with illegible phone numbers, six cans of tuna fish stuffed in a duffel bag, requited and unrequited lovers, lovers that quit before they got quited, those of you pondering major decisions, those of you who have already made your final major decision and changed it seven times, those looking around for someone who has an extra major decision to spare, those who are looking anxiously to the future, those who hope I keep speaking forever so that their future will be put on permanent hold, those who are smiling, those who are crying, those with sweaty palms and those with grim determination, birds, bees, bats, butterflies, and partly cloudy skies. Have I left anyone out? If you're not anywhere on the list I just mentioned, please see your faculty advisor to find out who and what you are. Chances are, you still need an extra two years here.

I am proud, honored, and delighted to be the commencement speaker for the Class of '84. Driving up here yesterday with road directions given to me by my daugh-

ter, I thought I would be the commencement speaker for the Class of '85. I realized as I passed signs that said "To Williams College," pointing left and pointing right simultaneously, that it is not enough just to graduate from this fine institution, it is not enough to receive a diploma, a degree, and a superb education — the most difficult part still lies ahead. You have got to find your way out of this place and try to get home.

I would, of course, like to extend my gratitude to the powers that be at Williams for graciously bestowing upon me an Honorary Doctorate in Letters. You must realize that honorary degrees are generally given to people whose SAT scores were too low to get them into the school the regular way. As a matter of fact, it was my SAT scores that led me into my present vocation in life — comedy. The last thing I am is ungrateful for this generous and gracious acknowledgment, but to be perfectly honest, I am not exactly sure what an honorary doctorate affords me in life. Am I now more intelligent or am I just honorarily smarter? Will I be invited to the homecoming games on the 50-yard line, or will I receive two honorary tickets which entitle me to listen to it on local radio? Actually, people with honorary awards are often looked upon with disfavor. Would you let an honorary mechanic fix your brand-new Mercedes? Now I have unwanted obligations. I feel that I now have to uphold the high esteem in which Williams is regarded in the academic world. Therefore,

when I learned a few months ago that I was going to receive this, I went out and read all of Proust and James
Joyce, and I discuss it passionately whenever I am with
groups of people. Unfortunately I am no longer invited to
parties and I have lost six of my closest friends. They now
refer to me as an Honorary Bore.

I have received other such awards, proudly. In 1981
Hofstra University awarded me an Honorary Doctor of
Humane Letters. To be frank, I thought a Humane Letter
was, "Dear Sir, we have decided not to kill your dog." In
1982 Cornell University made me an Honorary Bachelor
of Arts at Syracuse University. In 1983 Miami University
appointed me Dean of Arts and Sciences for the Fountain-
bleau Hotel. Princeton University gave me a chair. It was
one of those canvas wooden chairs that you use at the
beach. But it was from Princeton and they only charged
me $39.95, so I took it. I also gave two lectures at Harvard
University. I was not given any degrees or credits for it but
they did say it was worth the equivalent of forty-one lec-
tures at UCLA.

As fascinating as all that is, I am sure you graduates
are all sitting on the edge of your seats, waiting for the
words of wisdom that I have in a sealed envelope in my
breast pocket; words that will guide each and every one of
you happily and successfully through life — and for fifteen
special graduates whose names are in another sealed envelope inside the larger sealed envelope, special contacts in

various commercial fields that will guarantee you immediate jobs starting at a hundred thousand dollars a year. And for ten lucky women, special contacts that will guarantee immediate jobs starting at a hundred and fifty thousand dollars a year. I mean, if I was invited here to give advice, you might as well get something concrete.

I have given advice before. Four years ago I was the commencement speaker at my daughter's high school graduation in Los Angeles. To be honest, my advice to her and her fellow graduates was enlightening, informative, useful, direct, witty, charming, and most importantly, a fountain of knowledge, experience, and wisdom. But did she listen to my advice? Did she heed my words of wisdom? Of course not. That is why I am here today. Having to tell her the same damn thing all over again. That is why I hope when I soon give you graduates this priceless advice that will take all the pressures off you and open doors of opportunity everywhere, that you listen to every word I say. Because I do not want to have to rent a car and drive up here in 1988 just to repeat myself. If I have to come back again, all you are going to get from me is honorary advice. I am sure your parents are not going to be too pleased with that, especially since they are going to have to book their hotel rooms a year in advance again.

There was an elderly couple next door to me last night whose son graduated from Williams in 1944, but this was the first opening for a room they could get. They are

here today; he is not. He is sixty-five years old now and forgot what college he went to. The pity of it is he has not made much of his life since graduating from Williams. Why did he go wrong? I will tell you. Because on Graduation Day, he did not listen to the commencement speaker. Believe me, if I ran a college or a university, I would not waste time having a curriculum. I would not throw away good money hiring a faculty, buying important research equipment, and erecting new modernized buildings. I would just have four straight years of commencement speakers, and of course, one new motel with 23,000 rooms.

Hence we come to the reason we are gathered here today. We are gathered here today for me to tell you why we are gathered here today. Today you leave these hallowed halls, or, if you live off campus, your hallowed filthy rooms. From my years of experience, I can tell you it is not so important where you go once you leave Williams, but rather it is how you leave this remarkable institution. Therefore my first piece of sage advice is this: When you leave here today, it is vital that you take off those long black gowns. Very few businesses are going to hire someone applying for a job wearing a long black gown. Those who intend to go into medicine will find you will immediately lose your patients' confidence if you are examining them in a long black gown, wearing a pancake hat with a tassel hanging from it. Especially during operations. Patients coming out of sodium pentathol seeing a man over him wearing black

tend to have coronary occlusions. Future airplane pilots will discover passengers rushing for the exits when they see the captain getting into the cockpit in a long black gown, clutching a diploma. The only ones who should keep them on are those who intend to go into the long black gown business or those who intend to leave here and plan immediately to graduate from other colleges later this afternoon. The only other possible reason one might consider keeping their long black gowns on after graduation is if the label says Calvin Klein.

Advice number two: Upon leaving this day, do not tell any faculty member you think he is a creep. Faculty members have relatives everywhere. You do not want to enter law school and have your new professor say to you, "Oh, yes. My cousin Myron, the creep, told me to look out for you."

Advice number three: Do not take any classrooms with you. Mementoes are nice but leave the school the way you found it. Along this line, may I add, do not take home any girls who do not belong to you. For one thing, it is uncouth, and for another, she may be your employer one day.

Advice number four: When you return home to what you might call "civilian life" after four years away, there will be a certain period of adjustment. Williams, although not isolated, is certainly off the beaten track. Therefore, you might want to look around and notice how the styles

in clothing have changed since you left. People in big cities today tend not to wear their sweaters around their ankles. You do not have to completely drop the "casual" style of attire you have been used to, but you may want to start wearing shoes on the right foot as well as the left. Some of you women may consider giving your old clothes to the Salvation Army instead of buying from them.

Advice number five: Studies have proved that students returning home after four years away at college tend to get agoraphobia when having to sleep in a room with less than fourteen people in it. If it is difficult at first, sleep in a YMCA dormitory for a few days, then try a small hospital ward with four to six people until you feel you are ready to come back to a room of your own.

Advice number six: Do not take the very first job that is offered to you. Panic will only land you behind the counter at McDonald's. On the other hand, show some humility; do not walk into Chrysler Corporation and ask if they are looking for a replacement for Mr. Iacocca. Do not try to fake your way through an interview. If the vice president of I.B.M. wants to hire you as his secretary, tell him you cannot type. He will find out in a few weeks anyway. Be practical. Do not take any jobs that involve the handling of gorillas. Be cautious. Do not accept a position with any company that asks you to leave the head of a horse in someone's bed.

Advice number seven: You are not obligated to marry

the last person you had a date with. If you were foolish enough to make that promise, you can sneak off the grounds today quickly and quietly, wearing dark glasses and a false mustache. This applies both to men and women.

Advice number eight: Those who intend to enter the highly competitive business of writing poetry, do not expect to get rich quick. There is, of course, good money in poetry, but that is mostly because you save a good deal by not sending out your laundry or having to live in an apartment with heat.

Advice number nine: Those who played here at Williams and are contemplating a career in the National Football League — please think it over first. Not so much because you might get hurt — it is just that they may not have a uniform in your size.

Advice number ten: To put it bluntly, it is a dog-eat-dog world out there. Of course, one must seriously consider careers in such fields as silicone chips, laser beam technology, and space-age hardware. But I urge you to give some thought to the skills of artisans of the past, where hands labored in love and produced works of lasting beauty and enduring usefulness. These works are not only aesthetically rewarding but financially profitable as well. Look into blacksmithing. There are more openings today than there were a hundred years ago. Practice medicine by use of leeches. Once again, it is a wide-open field. Pyramid building. When was the last time you saw one go up?

And if it is travel and new cultures that interest you, what about looking for a shorter route to the West Indies? There are kings and queens in Spain who would pay big money for that.

And then there are the arts. There is not too much advice one can give to someone contemplating a life in the arts. One, of course, must have the talent, the gift, and the passion. Naturally, I try to tell young people to be born gifted, but you have to catch them early for that. Talent is the gift plus the passion. It is having a desire to succeed so intense that no force on earth can stop it. It takes years of discipline, sacrifice, and inspiration. No one in the world can give it to you. It can, however, be bought in small quantities from a handful of dealers in New York. Test it first before you give them any money. And Bloomingdale's occasionally carries it.

Through all the books I have read, all the plays and films and ballets I have seen, all the music I have listened to, there are just a few key bits of information that I can pass on to you, information that one day may prove invaluable. To budding painters, let me say one thing — and every art museum in the world will bear me out: Do not use too much red! It is a false color. I was on the Red Sea for ten days and never even noticed it. Think of how little red Picasso used during his Blue Period. It does, however, sometimes go well in bathrooms.

Music! Those of you who can bring us the har-

mony of music, the gaiety and sweetness of melody, bring peace, contentment, and serene joy to the world. We who listen to it are as heaven-blessed as those divine souls who bring it liltingly into our lives. Unless, of course, you play drums. To composers, there is only one true basic rule to follow: Try not to write music you have heard somewhere else. The lawsuits can wipe you out.

Literature. What I am about to say to you future novelists may seem crass and commercial, but it is the only way you can avoid going unheeded, unrecognized, and unread. If at all possible, get your Nobel Prize as soon as possible. Knock out those classics. Then call the Literary Guild and see how quickly they pick up the phone this time. Not to mention a nice little interview on *Good Morning, America.* You may even get invited to the White House, but if your books are truly profound, you will not have to go.

Playwriting. Playwrights are honorary novelists. It is a good life if you can stand the slings and arrows of criticism. Critics are honorary human beings. It is the question that is asked of me most frequently: what do I think of critics? I accept any review and judgment if I think it is honestly and intelligently written, without prejudice. There is, however, one critic who hates my plays two weeks before he goes to see them. He is surly, vicious, sadistic, cruel, and usually smells rather badly. He is always given three seats for opening night, two of which are unused, to

avoid anyone sitting next to him from getting up in the middle of the play to seek fresh air.

There is one last bit of advice I would like to leave you with, and for this we move into more sobering territory. In an effort to find a phrase or a word that I would like to pass on as inspirational, I thought about what best expressed the theme of my own life. It is a word I mentioned just a few moments before: passion! It is the force that has governed and motivated all my energies, that has given me the discipline that is mandatory in all creative efforts and that without it, life seems to me rather bleak and dismal.

In the play *Amadeus*, Salieri, the court composer, realizing young Mozart's genius when he hears his music for the first time, contemplates his own mediocre gifts by comparison and confides to the audience, "Is it enough just to have passion?" My daughter Nancy, who saw the play and was quite affected by it, talked to me about her own aspirations and, questioning her own abilities and talents, asked me the very same question. "Is it enough just to have a passion?" My answer was, "It is not only enough. It is everything." I have seen more talented and gifted people fail to attain their aspirations because of a lack of passion, which I can only describe as a flame that burns within us with such intense heat that it glows with a pure white light and cannot be extinguished by despair, misfortune, infirmity, or not being at home when an important phone call

comes in. Passion is the Super Bowl of enthusiasm. To have a passion for life is not only to wake up in the morning and hear birds singing, but it is taking the time to open the window to see where they are perched on the tree. That is one of the side benefits of passion. You pay attention to details. And it is the details that determine the quality of life.

It can be argued that passion is a luxury that none of us can afford. It is not necessary to have a passion for food to know what it is to be hungry. But it seems the ones who end up feeding us, nurturing us, teaching us, and loving us are the ones who are never devoid of passion. Their passion is the welfare of others.

More simply stated, whatever path you follow from the moment you hopefully take off those long black gowns, do it as though Gershwin had written music to underscore your every move. Romantic and idealistic, yes. But I cannot think of anything in life worthwhile that was achieved without a great desire to achieve it.

Basic Playwriting Rule Number One: The main character in your play has to want something and he has to want it ferociously. He has to want it in every act, every scene, every line of dialogue, whether it is in the text or subtext.

There is, to be fair, the flip side of passion. It is caution and timidity caused by an acute fear of failure. I can tell you from my own experience that the fear of failure is

infinitely greater than failure. Waiting with bated breath to hear the reviews on an opening night is torture. To finally hear the reviews, if they are favorable, is both joyous and unexpected. If they are negative, they are despairing and surprising. Surprising because although you may be despairing, you are also alive, breathing normally, drinking some Perrier and, with a little help from your friends, eating some pasta and a little chocolate mousse. In my own case, failure gets me up earlier the next morning than success. If you get right back to work, yesterday's pain becomes today's inspiration.

Do not confuse passion with success. Passion is the joy of getting there. Success can be a trap. I think this country and our culture glorifies and deifies the goddess Success to the point that whenever we try and fail, we hear our own inner voices say, "Shame upon you." If there is any shame, it is in the fact that we inflict such heavy punishment on ourselves. No world-ranking tennis player wants to be Number Two, no football coach would tolerate a loss in the playoffs (remember the phrase "Winning is everything"?). Television networks have late-night emergency meetings because their newest show was third in the ratings with only a paltry audience of thirty million viewers. Shame on them. Do not listen to that kind of thinking. There is probably not much thinking behind it anyway. Do not listen to those who say, "It is not done that way." Maybe it is not, but maybe you will. Do not listen to

those who say, "You're taking too big a chance." If he did not take a big chance, Michelangelo would have painted the Sistine floor and it would surely be rubbed out today. Most important, do not listen to yourself when the little voice of fear inside of you rears its ugly head and says, "They are all smarter than you out there. They are more talented, they are taller, blonder, prettier, luckier, and have connections. They have a cousin who took out Meryl Streep's baby-sitter." Give any credence at all to that voice, and your worst fears will surely come true. Do not turn over power so easily. Do not make those who speak with a louder voice automatically right. Respect is one thing, submission another. Walk into any situation in life — whether it is professional, artistic, competitive, or personal — with a lack of self-esteem and you have just turned over the upper hand to someone who may not have even asked for it. I firmly believe that if you follow a path that interests you — hopefully with a passion — and if you bring to it a sense of your own worth — not to the exclusion of love, sensitivity, and cooperation with others, but with the strength of conviction that you can move others by your own efforts — and do not make success or failure the criteria by which you live, the chances are you will be a person worthy of your own respect.

I do not know how much help I have given you today, but I can say this. For the privilege of letting me ad-

dress this gathering, what you have given me is a great deal of satisfaction. It has been years since I have had the opportunity to speak this long to my daughter without her interrupting. I have to amend that; she is the most interesting interrupter I have ever met. I am speaking as the father of Nancy right now, but in a sense, I am speaking for all the proud, happy, and tearful parents gathered here this morning, most of whom, unfortunately, probably missed breakfast.

To all you graduates, sending you off four years ago was a loss for us but a gain for Williams and yourselves. If I can say this without making it sound like a sentimental ballad, leaving here today is heading into another loss-and-gain situation. Saying good-bye to friends is a loss and saying hello to a world that appears to be filled with forbidding strangers does not seem to be much of a gain. But give it time. It has been working that way for millenniums, and aside from a few doomsayers and politicians, will continue to do so, at least until the grandchildren of this graduating class start writing for their rooms a year in advance. If you have lost anything here at Williams, I hope it is nothing more than the green scarf your Aunt Blanche gave you the day you left home. What you have gained, I am more than certain is something more precious, more valuable, and more unforgettable than even finding that shorter route to the West Indies.

I thank you for inviting me. I thank you for my honorary doctorate. I intend to make house calls and will be on vacation in August. I will now heed my own advice and take off this long black gown. I am going to a wedding this evening and do not want to be confused with the mother of the bride. Thank you.

GLORIA STEINEM

Gloria Steinem is one of the most influential writers, editors, and activists of our time. She travels extensively as a lecturer and feminist organizer and is a frequent spokesperson on issues of equality. In the late 1960's, she became a major feminist leader, and in 1972, she co-founded *Ms.* magazine, an international feminist bimonthly, where she serves as consulting editor. She is the author of several books, including *Revolution From Within: A Book of Self-Esteem*, which topped best-seller lists in the United States and other English-speaking countries. Steinem helped found the Woman's Action Alliance and the National Woman's Political Caucus. She was born in 1934 in Toledo, Ohio.

GLORIA STEINEM

Tufts University
Medford, Massachusetts
May 17, 1987

Just in case the honor of this company and this occasion might endanger my humility, here is a note of reality: I do not remember one single thing my own commencement speaker said. I was consumed with concern about how my friends would get on with my family, and vice versa, about how I was going to pack four years of possessions in one car, and about how I was not going to get married to the very tempting man I was then engaged to. In the fifties, everybody got married or engaged before or right after graduation — but I wanted to go off to India instead.

Furthermore, I conducted a small survey in preparation for today. Half of my sample could not remember who their commencement speaker was.

So instead of pursuing one theme that might exclude many people, I am going to be diverse in the hope of leaving a sentence or two that might be useful to more people. All these thoughts come under the general heading of "What I Know Now That I Wish I Had Known Then." One other organizing principle I will leave to the end — and I defy you to guess what it is. I have also tried to follow Henny Youngman's wisdom — he always told one-

221

liners because longer jokes were not, as he put it, "worth the trip" — by keeping each thought short.

Thought 1: A person who has experienced something is almost always far more expert on it than are the experts. A corollary is that any process including only experts, with no contribution from those with personal experience, will probably go wrong. An extension is that our educational system is long on book learning, but short on apprenticeship. A further extension is that our social policy is long on theorists and short on organizers.

A national example: The poverty programs of the Johnson Administration were less successful than the Depression projects of the Roosevelt Administration, in part because the first were mostly designed by Washington "poverticians," while the second were mostly local initiatives that were given government support.

For a personal example: I wish someone had warned me that book learning, as valuable and irreplaceable as it may be, can also make you self-critical, reverential, and otherwise fearful of acting. Of course, this is especially true if you are female, or a different race or ethnicity, and nobody in the books looks like you — but I hope you have had more inclusive textbooks than I did.

So whatever you want to do, just do it. Do not worry about making a fool of yourself. Making a damn fool of yourself is absolutely essential. And you will have a great time.

Thought 2: When I was a student, we used to sit around discussing whether a particular end justified a particular means. On the assumption of everyone from Marx or Machiavelli, I thought that was the question.

It took me twenty years to figure out that the means are the ends — and vice versa. Whatever means you use, become an organic part of the ends you achieve.

For example: Groups rarely benefit from revolutions if they have not been an organic part of that revolution. Even if they are given certain paper rights at the end of the process, they may remain too weak to use them. Strength comes from process. Process is all.

Thought 3: If you have to choose character or intelligence — in a friend or in a candidate — choose character. Intelligence without character is dangerous, but character without intelligence only slows down a good result.

Thought 4: Politics is not just what goes on in the electoral system or in Washington. Politics is any power relationship in our daily lives. Anytime one human being is habitually powerful over another, or one group over another, not because of talent or experience but just because of race, or sex, or class, that is politics. So when we look at the fields of your state and mind and see that one color of human being owns them and another color works on them as migrant labor, that is politics. When we find a hundred of one kind of human being in the typing pool and a few of another in the boardroom, that is politics. When chil-

dren have only their father's name, that is politics. When most men have only one job, while most women have two — one inside the home and one outside it — that is politics, too. And when students of color are still in smaller proportion than are people of color in the population, or women are a lesser percentage of dentists and engineers, or men a lesser proportion of physical therapists and nutritionists, that is politics.

Forget old definitions. They were based on the idea that what happened to men was politics, and what happened to women was culture. That division was just a way of keeping certain parts of life immune to change. In fact, the personal is very often political. And revolutions, like houses, get built from the bottom up, not the top down.

Thought 5: As Margaret Mead once said, "Marriage worked well in the nineteenth century because people only lived to be fifty."

Because life expectancy has increased about thirty years since 1900, there are bound to be different ways of living. Some people will marry and raise children young, then go off amicably for another life or a different accomplishment. Some will marry late — after their work lives are well under way — and have children later or not at all. Some will not marry or will love and live with a partner of the same gender. Others will raise their children among a chosen family of friends or find colleagues in work and shared ideals who are their spiritual family.

As the prison of form diminishes, we can pay more attention to content. That means equal power between partners and thus the possibility of free choice. That means commitment out of decision, not desperation or pressure. That means kindness, empathy, and nurturing — because those of us who are not parents can help those who are. We can have children as friends.

If that sounds Polllyanna-ish, consider that the foreshadowings of such a change are with us now. Women in the paid workforce — and hopefully men who are real parents, too — are finally beginning to bring the reality of children's lives into the public sphere. This is long overdue: The United States is the only industrialized democracy in the world that behaves as if children did not exist until the age of six.

Furthermore, the divorce rate has begun to decline, an event that feminists have always predicted. When people used to say to me, "Feminism is the cause of divorce," I always said, "No, marriage is the cause of divorce." Forcing all people to believe they had to live one way was the cause of many bad marriages, just as forcing all people to believe they had to be parents was the cause of many bad parents and unhappy children. No one way of living can be right for all people.

So the message is: Do not worry if your life does not look like a Dick-and-Jane primer. Do not worry if it does not look like the yuppy opposite of a Dick-and-Jane

primer. The point is less what we choose than that we have the power to make a choice.

Thought 6: Remember the fifties and sixties? Then, women were supposed to marry what we wanted to become — as in, "Marry a doctor, don't be one." In the seventies and eighties, some women started to say, "We are becoming the men we wanted to marry." But in the nineties, more men must become the women they wanted to marry.

I will know we are getting someplace when as many young men as young women ask, "How can I combine career and family?"

And men will be getting someplace, too. They will not be strangers to their children anymore. They will not be suppressing qualities in themselves that are human but not stereotypically masculine. They will even be living longer, since the pressures of having to win, or even be aggressive or violent, all lead to the clear conclusion that the prison of the so-called masculine role is the killer of many men.

This is not a role exchange — it's a humanization of both roles. For both women and men, progress probably lies in the direction we have not been. For women, it may lie in becoming more active in public life. For men, it may lie in playing a real part of private life. But for both, the pleasure and reward is becoming a whole human being.

I wish I had realized this earlier. It means that

progress is not always a straight line, in which we must defeat or outstrip others and there is only one winner. Progress is a circle in which we strive to use all our talents and complete ourselves. Potentially, we are all winners.

Thought 7: Do not forget to give at least ten percent of everything you earn to social change. It is the best investment you will ever make. Possessions can be lost, broken, or begin to possess you. Indeed, if you are really happy in your life and work, you will not have that much time to shop and buy and rebuy and repair anyway. The money you save may not be worth that much tomorrow. Insurance companies may cancel your policies. Tithing is the pioneer example and the religious example. Helping others is the only way to be sure there will be someone there to help you.

Finally, the last thought and an organizing principle of this list of I-wish-I-had-knowns: the reason why acting on such thoughts is timely and vital right now.

Economists are warning and politicians are fearing that this nation is at the end of its economic expansionist period. There are now other countries that can compete or even outstrip us in productivity. For the first time, eighty percent of Americans have not increased their real buying power in the last ten years, and many young people will not do as well in conventional economic terms as their parents.

Most authorities see this as a time of danger — and

that is true. Energies deflected from earning more and buying more could cause us to fly apart politically. But this is also an opportunity to make real changes in our lives and in our country. It is time for America to become known for the quality of life as well as the quantity of goods.

It is time to carry out the greatest mission and legacy of our culture: that we are the world's biggest experiment in multicultural and multiracial living. Our fragile planet needs to learn exactly this lesson of cherishing each other's differences. This campus is imperfect, but it is far better than the world outside it, and the world could be much more like it — with politicians as open to visitors as are the deans in the hall I face, women heading newspapers and governments as they do here, and commitment to mutual support and nonviolence.

Bigger is not better. America's military might is not our best legacy.

Equality is the best insurance against the political upheaval that authorities fear. More than seventy percent of Americans say they are willing to change their standard of living in conventional economic terms — providing this so-called "sacrifice" is evenly spread.

This is a turning point in history — and your challenge. Our hearts go with you. Our heads and hands are here to help you. The brotherhood of man and the sisterhood of women — the humanity of people — is "not so

wild a dream as those who profit by delaying it would have us believe."

One more point. This is the last period of time that will seem lengthy to you at only three or four years. From now on, time will pass without artificial academic measure. It will go by like the wind. Whatever you want to do, do it now. For life is time, and time is all there is.

PHOTO CREDITS

PERMISSIONS